TERESA DURYEA WONG

MAGIC *and* MEMORIES

45 YEARS OF INTERNATIONAL QUILT FESTIVAL

AISLE 900

AISLE 800

AISLE 700

AISLE 600

1 Yard Kits

Queen & King Kits

Mini Bundles

ENGLAND DESIGN
Dickinson, Texas

SCHIFFER PUBLISHING

4880 Lower Valley Road • Atglen, PA 19310

Other Schiffer Books by the Author:
Japanese Contemporary Quilts and Quilters: The Story of an American Import, ISBN 978-0-7643-4874-7
Cotton & Indigo from Japan, ISBN 978-0-7643-5351-2

Other Schiffer Books on Related Subjects:
Art Quilts Unfolding: 50 Years of Innovation, Sandra Sider, ISBN 978-0-7643-5626-1
Art Quilts International: Abstract & Geometric, Martha Sielman, ISBN 978-0-7643-5220-1
HERstory Quilts: A Celebration of Strong Women, Susanne Miller Jones, ISBN 978-0-7643-5460-1

Designed by Molly Shields
Cover design by Brenda McCallum

Type set in Adorn Bouquet/Adobe Garamond Pro

Cover image: Cynthia England. *Show Time*. 2018. Cotton: 39" × 35" (99 × 89 cm). Machine quilted.

This quilt is based on a photograph and made with a technique known as picture piecing. Cynthia graciously agreed to create this commission for the cover of this book. The word Texas appears 14 times; 34 different quilts from Cynthia's collection are included; and the quilt was made with approximately 4,000 individual pattern pieces. Karey Patterson Bresenhan and Nancy O'Bryant Puentes are featured in the quilt.

Dedication page image: Judy Coates Perez. *Polychromatic Predilection*. 2017. 40" × 40" (102 × 102 cm).

Back cover images:
Top left: Karey Patterson Bresenhan and Nancy O'Bryant Puentes. *Photo by Ira Strickstein,* The Houston Post
Top right: Inside the International Quilt Festival.
Bottom left: Ted Storm-van Weelden. *Nocturnal Garden* (detail). 2001.
Bottom right: Jean Biddick. *Looking High and Low*. 2004. Cotton: 81" × 81" (206 × 206 cm).

Photo credits: Kim Coffman. Bob Ruggiero. Rhianna Griffin. Steve Campbell. Richard Cunningham. Jimmy Wong. King Chou Wong. Mary Stallings. Gensler. Teresa Duryea Wong.

ISBN: 978-0-7643-5741-1
Printed in China

Published by Schiffer Publishing, Ltd.
4880 Lower Valley Road
Atglen, PA 19310
Phone: (610) 593-1777; Fax: (610) 593-2002
E-mail: Info@schifferbooks.com
Web: www.schifferbooks.com

For our complete selection of fine books on this and related subjects, please visit our website at www.schifferbooks.com. You may also write for a free catalog.

Schiffer Publishing's titles are available at special discounts for bulk purchases for sales promotions or premiums. Special editions, including personalized covers, corporate imprints, and excerpts, can be created in large quantities for special needs. For more information, contact the publisher.

We are always looking for people to write books on new and related subjects. If you have an idea for a book, please contact us at proposals@schifferbooks.com.

Dedicated to quilters everywhere

Once a year, tens of thousands of women—and quite a few men—undergo a pilgrimage to Houston, Texas. They return year after year. Nothing but the most dire of circumstances could keep them away. Their destination? The International Quilt Festival—an enormous confluence of exhibitions, shopping, competitions, educational opportunities, and, most importantly, a gathering of kindred spirits like no other.

For one wonderful week, the doors open and the magic begins. A magic that has been transforming and inspiring countless quilters and would-be quilters for 45 years.

"I feel like I've died and gone to heaven," attendees said over and over as they entered the 2014 Festival and saw the stunning exhibit *Ruby Jubilee: A 40-Year Celebration*. The pinnacle was an enormous circular display of quilts hanging from the ceiling.

CONTENTS

PREFACE

It's difficult to express to outsiders the deep connection—the calling—that we quilters feel to Festival. It's also difficult to communicate just how profoundly the experience changes the quilter and the quilts she will make. This preface is the story of how Festival has changed my own life. If you take my story and change the names, you will have the story of tens of thousands of other quilters who've had similar transformative experiences. My story is their story.

My quilt buddy Amy Gurghigian introduced me to the International Quilt Festival in 1999. Amy and I lived down the street from each other, and we met when our daughters were in the same fourth-grade class. Once I visited her home and saw her artistic collection of handmade quilts, I asked her to teach me how to quilt. Pretty soon, I was hooked. For us, attending Festival every year is a given. Wild horses could not keep us away.

Each and every year, Amy and I enter Festival on opening night during a special two-hour preview for students. This is a perfect time to breeze up and down the aisles before the crowds. Amy has very specific booths that she must visit, and many a Preview Night I've followed alongside her—walking at a mighty brisk pace—directly to certain booths to be first in line to buy special goods that sell out quickly, such as scrap bags of hand-dyed wool. After the commotion of the opening night subsides, I take a more leisurely pace and walk up and down the aisles, day after day. There is no way to absorb it all in only one pass. In my early years at Festival, I was always collecting specific fabrics and building my stash. I was (and still am) very picky about my choices, and I wanted only certain styles of fabric. These were the days before internet shopping, so collecting special fabric required patience, but Festival brought it right to us quilters all at once.

My life as a working mom, wife, daughter, and quilter was a never-ending balancing act. As soon as one Festival ended and the dates for the upcoming year were announced, I would add those dates to my calendars immediately. All year, I made sure nothing interfered with Festival. It wasn't always easy, though.

For many years, Amy and I faced two very dramatic annual deadlines related to our Festival adventure. One was to register for classes. When the catalog for the International Quilt Festival was mailed out around the first of July every year (pre-internet days), Amy and I would sit down together and choose a class. We needed to register right away because the best classes filled fast. We studied with Noriko Endo, Karen Kay Buckley, Caryl Bryer Fallert-Gentry, Hollis Chatelain, and others. These are some of the rock stars of the quilt world. We cherished those classes and always went home filled with new ideas and better quiltmaking skills.

The other frantic deadline was trying to get a hotel room. Even though we lived in the Houston suburbs, we chose to stay in a hotel, since Houston traffic is notorious and parking downtown is not free. While many more hotels operate downtown these days, in the first decade of the twenty-first century there were only so many rooms available at the adjoining Hilton Americas. The Hilton would release rooms for Festival on a certain day, usually in early January. I always felt the thrill of victory when we scored one of the coveted rooms. We just loved the camaraderie of staying overnight next to the convention center along with thousands of other quilters. In 2017, the Houston agency that tracks hotel occupancy rates recorded 13,029 nights of hotel stays in downtown Houston (host hotels) during Market and Festival. That's a lot of rooms booked for one event, especially considering the fact that the majority of quilters share a room.

There were no husbands and no kids. No chores. No work. We were free to truly experience Festival for a couple of days inside a hotel filled with "our people." In the evenings, hotel room doors were propped open and women waltzed in and out of each other's rooms, showing off their purchases, studying the prizes others found, and strategizing for the next

day's hunt. There was laughter and talking into the wee hours of the night. In fact, I was always one to go to sleep early, and one year I begged Amy to go out into the hall and tell the women to be quiet. Luckily, she refused, and we laughed about it later.

There are around a thousand booths at Festival, selling fabric, books, tools, patterns, kits, clothing, beads, lace, baskets, quilt furniture, and so on. The biggie purchases are the machines. I ended up buying two machines at Festival, both from Bernina. The first one was a quilting machine. Prior to this, I had used a Kenmore sewing machine that I purchased from Sears for a couple hundred bucks. The Bernina was a whole new category! I took out a five-year, interest-free payment plan to buy it. Machine quilting has unleashed a ton of new ideas and ways to create quilts. I owe the discovery of this machine and the way it has affected my creative life to Festival.

One day as I was walking the exhibition aisles of Festival, I rounded a corner and saw a large quilt, an almost all-white snowy scene, with a dog and a fence. That quilt was made by David Taylor, and it stopped me in my tracks. I just thought it was so beautiful and so painterly. I signed up for an all-day Festival class taught by him on an appliqué technique. I was in the middle of a busy work project, but I convinced my boss to give me the day off. It turned out that wasn't such a good idea—he ended up calling me every hour and I had to keep stepping out of the classroom to take his calls. Even though I missed a lot of the instruction that day, I was especially interested in his technique, and years later I took a four-day art quilt retreat with David. It's because of Festival that I learned of him, as well as dozens of other profoundly influential quilters and teachers. Seeing his quilt inspired the all-day Festival class, the retreat, and eventually a quilt of my own. I entered my quilt in a special juried exhibition at Festival titled *It's Raining Cats and Dogs* (2014). When I was notified that my quilt was accepted, I was elated, and I owe that entire journey to Festival.

Teresa Duryea Wong (*center*) at the Texas Quilt Museum with Karey Patterson Bresenhan (*left*) and Nancy O'Bryant Puentes. In 2014, she was named the first Bybee Scholar.

It was at Festival that I first discovered Japanese quilts, beginning with those of Noriko Endo, Yoko Saito, and Keiko Goke. The styles of these quilters are vastly different, yet each has affected me in special ways. I distinctly remember walking the exhibitor aisles and coming upon the booth hosted by Yoko Saito and her company, Quilt Party. Everything in her booth featured a taupe palette, and I'd never seen anything quite like it. I was instantly drawn in. I first became a groupie of the Japanese aesthetic, then a serious researcher, then an author of two books on Japanese quilts and textiles. That passion was born at Festival!

My Festival journey morphed into professional opportunity when I was invited to give a lecture in 2017. But even though I now have a role as a researcher and author, I am still a quilter. Amy and I still attend Festival together. We still hunt for fabric. We still get giddy when it's time for the special two-hour preview slot on opening night. And most of all, we still feel the magic of this event that calls us year after year.

I first met Festival founder Karey Patterson Bresenhan and her cousin Nancy O'Bryant Puentes when they presented me the honor of being named the first "Bybee Scholar" on behalf of the Faith P. and Charles L. Bybee Foundation and the Texas Quilt Museum. I knew who they were, of course, but had never met them prior to this event. Later on, I began to learn the story of how they created this incredibly transformative event. I once asked them if they fully realized the impact Festival has had on the lives of quilters. They nodded and said yes, yes, of course, but I got the feeling they might be so busy working on the "day to dayness" of it all that perhaps they didn't totally recognize the story of how ordinary quilters like me have been transformed by Festival.

I felt strongly that their story was one that needed to be told. I began a long, private campaign to convince Nancy and Karey to allow me to tell their story. They were hesitant at first, mostly because of modesty and privacy concerns. But more importantly, they hesitated because most people do not think their own story is all that interesting, Karey and Nancy included. The upcoming forty-fifth anniversary of Festival was the winning ticket that helped propel us to reach an agreement to share this important story.

I spent four years (off and on) researching this book. During this time, I had the good fortune to formally interview Karey and Nancy during thirteen long sessions at their homes. I'm beyond grateful for their trust in me to write this book, and for the time they invested talking with me and sharing their story. I hope you enjoy reading it and reliving the past forty-five years of this magical event we call Festival.

Teresa Duryea Wong

ACKNOWLEDGMENTS

I am forever grateful to my fellow Texans, Karey Patterson Bresenhan and Nancy O'Bryant Puentes, for building the International Quilt Festival and this industry I love. Their tenacity and dogged determination have had an enormous impact on the lives of many thousands of ordinary quilters. This book would not have been possible without the talent and experience of Bob Ruggiero—the guy who can name a quilt, any quilt, in under two seconds. I'm also grateful to Judy Murrah for her sincere encouragement. She would have been proud to see this book completed. My Austin friends Katherine J. Adams, Kathy Moore, and Suzanne Labry provided support throughout the long research days and were the first readers of this manuscript. I'm endlessly grateful to my friend, my first quilt teacher, and the woman who first introduced me to Festival, Amy Gurghigian. Last, but most importantly, my photographer husband, Jimmy Wong, has listened to more quilt stories than he ever imagined, and he even climbed the rafters of the giant convention center to take spectacular photos of the whole crazy scene. He also spent countless hours scanning and enhancing old photos and along the way provided a ton of loving support.

Karey Patterson Bresenhan (*left*) and Nancy O'Bryant Puentes on October 15, 1991, inside Great Expectations quilt shop in Houston, Texas, which Karey owned and operated for many years. They're wrapped in the quilt titled *The Founders' Star*, pieced by Karey's mother, Jewel Pearce Patterson, and quilted by Marge Weisheit. *Photo by Ira Strickstein,* The Houston Post

PART ONE

The Magic

For one wonderful week, the doors open and the magic of the International Quilt Festival begins.

Introduction

Houston: Quilt Central

New York and Los Angeles have Wall Street and Hollywood. Houston has quilts! Well, that and oil, medicine, and NASA. Houston is the energy capital of the world, and there are a plethora of oil and gas companies operating in the city with hundreds of thousands of employees who live there. Besides energy, Houston is also home to the renowned Texas Medical Center and NASA's Johnson Space Center. Houston is complex, sprawling, and diverse. Yet, when millions of people around the world think of Houston, they think of quilts. That's because the country's fourth-largest city is home to the biggest quilting event in the Western world: the International Quilt Festival.

On the eastern edge of the city's downtown district sits the George R. Brown Convention Center. The front facade of this huge facility faces the shiny city skyline. The GRB opened in 1987 and became the permanent home of the International Quilt Festival that same year.

It's named after George Rufus Brown (1898–1983), a wealthy oilman and philanthropist, and the younger brother of Herman Brown, who was one of the founders of Brown and Root, a large oil services company. George became a partner of Brown and Root in 1923, and in the 1930s he helped found and lead a group of bankers and millionaire oilmen who were instrumental in planning for Houston's growth. George personally stepped up and donated land—specifically, six of the eleven blocks needed—to build a new downtown convention center.

When the doors open on this massive, 1.8-million-square-foot center, quilters rarely think about old George Rufus and his plans for Houston way back then. Their thoughts are focused on how to navigate the center and whether they wore the right shoes! Just how big is 1.8 million square feet? Well, the American football field is 360 feet (110 meters) long and 160 feet (49 meters) wide, which is 57,600 square feet. That means that thirty-one football fields could fit inside all three floors of the GRB! That's a lot of convention floor to cover for the intrepid quilter.

Each year, approximately sixty thousand people descend on the George R. Brown Convention Center in downtown Houston to attend this magical week of quilts, classes, shopping, exhibitions, and quiltmaking. They come from all over the United States and some forty countries.

Aerial view of the city of Houston. *Photo by Carol M. Highsmith, courtesy of Wikimedia Commons*

A City for Quilts

When quilters first enter the International Quilt Festival, they are greeted by an enormous explosion of color and an insanely busy hub of energy and enthusiasm. One can see quilts and quilters in every direction, and a flood of opportunities await. It is a magical, temporary city built solely for the love of quilts.

Behind the scenes, Festival operations are in fact equivalent to the operations of a small city. There is a shopping district, a museum district, and a quilting academy equal in size to a small junior college. There is a full-time security force and full-time medical aid on site. A huge food court inside the center and dozens of nearby restaurants support this city of quilts. Transportation is

In 2017, quilters in the US spent a whopping $3.76 billion on their fiber arts. Many of the most unique and high-quality products are offered at more than a thousand booths at the International Quilt Festival.

also available for multiple day trips outside the GRB to regional quilt shops and other venues, and shuttle buses are ready to transport quilters to and from downtown hotels.

Organizing this activity requires year-round planning, and that's where Quilts Inc. comes in. Quilts Inc. is the parent company that owns and operates International Quilt Festival, as well as International Quilt Market (the industry's only wholesale trade show for quilt shops) and other shows. A second International Quilt Festival is held in Chicago in the spring, and International Quilt Market's spring shows are held in major cities around the US. Quilts Inc. has a small, dedicated staff of around twenty employees who work on a myriad of tasks all year preparing for Festival and Market. The team is led by Karey Patterson Bresenhan, president and CEO, who founded Quilts Inc. in 1979, and Nancy O'Bryant Puentes, executive vice president. The captivating story of how these two tenacious women changed the course of quilt history is revealed in the second half of this book.

Festival activity kicks off on a Monday morning in late October or early November with a full-fledged quiltmaking academy. Over 550 classes and lectures are available during the week. This academy is so expansive that it takes up most of the third floor of the convention center. Instructors are carefully selected from among the most-experienced and popular applicants. Each year, individuals who aspire to teach must submit a detailed application that describes the type of instruction they offer and their teaching or lecturing experience. This is *not* the place for newbie teachers. The 150 or so instructors who are ultimately chosen are usually well established, and many quilters know their work and quilting style. Classes will fill up quickly. Oftentimes, quilters will travel long distances just for the opportunity to study with a certain teacher. Festival offers those quilters a wide selection of the "best of the best" instructors all in one place. In 2017, this famed quiltmaking academy hit a new record of five thousand registered students.

The quiltmaking academy offers just about every type of quilting style available, with varying levels of skill required. A beginning quilter can learn basic sewing and block construction, and the most advanced quilter can learn specialized techniques of hand-dyed fabric or painting with thread, or even how to use high-tech long-arm quilting machines. There are classes for appliqué techniques, improvisational construction, machine embroidery, and many other options as well.

Doors open for the main Festival activities on Wednesday night, known as the Preview Night, and the show continues through Sunday afternoon. The main floor of the gigantic

GRB is divided into two halves: shopping and exhibition space. The shopping half is by far the biggest attraction for Festival attendees. Over a thousand booths line the aisles, and shoppers can find fabric galore, tools of all types, sewing and quilting machines, books, patterns, quilt kits, and many other quilting products. In addition, there are handmade quilts and antique quilts for sale. Other booths offer clothing, jewelry, lace, beads, baskets, etc. Many exhibitors make and sell quilt-sewing tables and chairs, as well as cabinets and display racks.

During peak hours, the shopping aisles are packed full of women and a few men. The quilters come prepared, and most carry sensible bags to hold their purchases as comfortably as possible. Many of the favorite booths will be filled wall to wall with shoppers, and there are often lines at the cash registers. In fact, some savvy quilters will notify their credit card companies in advance that they are attending an event with international vendors and will be making multiple purchases. Otherwise, some credit card security procedures will cut off their cards as they see charges from exhibitor companies from locations as diverse as North Carolina, England, and Japan in rapid succession.

Some exhibitor booths are tiny spaces with just enough room to highlight specialized products. Other booths occupy multiple spaces and have a large inventory and snazzy signage, sometimes high above the show floor and visible from every direction. Essentially all the major brands in the quilt world are represented in the booths, such as Moda, RJR, Hoffman Fabrics, FreeSpirit, Bernina, Janome, Brother, Baby Lock, Superior, Handi Quilter, Innova, Hobbs, and so many others. In addition to the big brands, small business owners also come to Festival, and inside their booths quilters will discover unusual products such as artisan hand-dyed fabric, innovative fusible and adhesive products, fancy irons, an endless variety of scissors, and even antique lace or hand-crafted thimbles. Some exhibitors offer patterns and kits to make complete quilts, and a few booths are even geared toward garment sewing or home decorating.

The shopping area also offers a steady stream of free demonstrations. Some are impromptu demos on specific machines, tools, or techniques. Others are scheduled demos by well-known quilters, and many attendees will crowd around to see these quick instruction sessions.

Alongside the shopping hub is the exhibition space, where more than 1,600 quilts and fabric art creations are on display. Throughout its forty-five-year history, Festival has placed an extraordinary amount of attention on the quality of its quilt exhibitions. Each quilt is professionally hung by experienced and specially trained teams, and the entire exhibition space, with its subdued lighting, quiet aisles, and carpeted floors, has an atmosphere equal to a fine-art museum.

Attending Festival is an annual pilgrimage for tens of thousands of quilters.

More than one hundred volunteers arrive on the designated setup day to help hang the thousand-plus quilts. Some of these volunteers return year after year. The most-elite and highly trained volunteers form an invitation-only group known as the Piece Corps. This group, which has about twenty active members, works alongside Festival staff on the most-delicate work.

In addition, there are another two hundred volunteers whose duties include assisting with safeguarding the exhibitions, helping attendees figure out where to go, and staffing the Festival information desk, among other duties.

Over the years, Festival has hosted numerous groundbreaking and innovative quilt exhibitions alongside beautiful displays

Andi Perejda. *1910 Revisited.*
2000. Cotton: 81" × 81"
(206 × 206 cm).
Machine pieced, hand appliqué,
hand quilted.

This beautiful red-and-white
quilt is an elaborate
reproduction of a kaleidoscope
quilt originally made in 1910 by
an unknown quiltmaker.
*Courtesy of International Quilt
Festival Collection*

of antique and contemporary quilts. Quilts that contain political statements or exude strong emotional expressions can sometimes be exhibited around the corner from illustrated or painted quilts, or even exhibits featuring traditional, gorgeous floral appliqué.

The juried competition of the International Quilt Association (IQA)—called "Quilts: A World of Beauty"—is one of the most popular exhibitions each year. Quilters are anxious to see the winning entries, and their first priority is to walk along the front aisle where the top winners are exhibited. Quilts are made by members of IQA and can be submitted annually in more than twenty different categories. All the prizes include a cash award and are nonpurchase prizes, which means that all winning quilts are returned to the maker. The cash award for Best of Show is $12,500. The top eight awards include a cash prize and hotel and airfare to and from Festival. In rare cases, a few quilters will choose to offer their quilts for sale during Festival, and IQA will help facilitate the purchase.

In addition to the annual IQA exhibits, there are many other exhibits on view, some of which are organized by Festival staff. Outside organizations can also make special arrangements for exhibitions. For example, the Studio Art Quilt Associates hosts juried exhibits annually of art quilts made by their members, and, like IQA, some of the SAQA quilts are also available for sale. Sometimes quilt guilds from around the state of Texas organize displays of quilts from their talented members. Authors, researchers, artists, or curators might also arrange for special exhibitions of quilts that are collected especially for a new book or to highlight a particular group of quilters or quilts.

Jean Biddick. *Looking High and Low*. 2004. Cotton: 81" × 81" (206 × 206 cm). Machine pieced, hand quilted.

Many viewers assume that the intricate center of this original quilt is appliqué, but it is expertly pieced instead. The design is based on the premise of standing at the base of a beautiful, historic European church tower and looking up. Thousands of pieces of fabric, each lined up perfectly, were used to create a three-dimensional-looking border and a thrilling center piece. It was awarded First Place, Innovative Pieced, Large, sponsored by Omnigrid, 2004.

Forty-Five Years of Memorable Exhibitions and Highlights from International Quilt Festival

Each year, there are approximately forty-five different exhibitions on view at one time. The following is only a small sample of quilt exhibitions over the years. Please note, this list does not include the annual IQA exhibit. However, images of many of the winning IQA quilts are featured throughout this book.

1975
Great Expectations

First event held at Great Expectations, an antique store owned by Karey Patterson Bresenhan.
Antique quilts were displayed and sold.
The public was invited to attend.

1976
River Oaks Garden Club Forum of Civics

Karey Patterson Bresenhan and her mother, Jewel Patterson, cofounded the Quilt Guild of Greater Houston and signed up the first twenty-five members at the show.
For the next four years, Karey volunteered to organize annual quilt fairs under the umbrella of the QGGH.
First year to include multiple exhibitors, in addition to Great Expectations.

1977
St. Paul's United Methodist Church, Fellowship Hall

Twice as much exhibition space as previous venue.
A fashion show that featured a woman wearing a handmade patchwork bikini made some attendees blush, including a few Amish visitors.

1978
St. Luke's Methodist Church, Gymnasium

The first judged quilt show.
New venue allowed quilts to hang from the ceiling.

1979
St. Luke's Methodist Church, Gymnasium

An outstanding exhibit of Grace Snyder's remarkable quilts, including her most famous quilt, *Flower Basket Petit Point*, made in 1942–43.

1980
Shamrock Hilton

Karey Patterson Bresenhan, owner and founder of Quilts Inc., hosted the first Quilt Festival in the fabled Shamrock Hilton hotel.

Quintessential Quilts: Thirty-five contemporary quilts, each a state winner from the national contest sponsored by *Good Housekeeping*, the US Historical Society, and the Museum of American Folk Art. The Smithsonian Institution coordinated multiple venues for this exhibition to travel throughout the US.

Almost life-size quilt featuring American football star Earl Campbell draws large crowds and becomes an icon.

1981
Shamrock Hilton

Crib Quilts: Small and Wonderful: Collection of antique baby quilts organized by Thomas K. Woodard and Blanche Greenstein of New York, authors of *Crib Quilts*.

1982
Shamrock Hilton

Eight thousand attendees from all over the US as well as Canada, Japan, and Australia.

Over two thousand antique and contemporary quilts offered for sale by exhibitors from many different regions.

1983
Shamrock Hilton

Exhibition of heirloom quilts from the Depression era.

1984

Shamrock Hilton

Quilt National: A landmark cooperative agreement between Festival and Quilt National brought to the show thirty extraordinary art quilts made by contemporary quiltmakers.

1985

Shamrock Hilton

Hands All Around: Debut of an annual exhibition that included quilts from Australia, Brazil, Canada, Denmark, England, France, Greece, India, Ireland, Japan, New Zealand, Norway, Scotland, South Africa, Switzerland, Tahiti, and West Germany.

Remember Me: Friendship Quilts: Twenty antique quilts from the nineteenth century made in traditional Friendship Album style. These "dated treasures" showcased the wonderful printed cottons available to nineteenth-century quiltmakers.

Nancy O'Bryant Puentes coordinated a landmark quilt conservation seminar as part of the Texas Quilt Search, the first in the nation to bring together professional textile conservators, museum textile curators and staff, and quilt artists to establish a dialogue about the importance of preserving quilt and textile art. Based on Nancy's efforts and the publication of her book *First Aid for Family Quilts*, an educational quilt care and conservation display was introduced and became a then-regular part of Festival. The Austin Area Quilt Guild organized this initially, then later the Bay Area Quilt Guild took it over.

1986

Albert Thomas Convention Center

This was the first year Festival adopted the slogan "World's Fair of Quilts," which came from a *Southern Living* magazine article about the show.

Hands All Around II: Magnificent display of quilts from makers around the world. Quilts are featured in a new book, *Hands All Around: Quilts from Many Nations* (New York: E. P. Dutton, 1987), by Robert Bishop (d. 1991), director of the Museum of American Folk Art, New York; Karey Patterson Bresenhan, founder/owner Quilts Inc., and International Quilt Festival; and Bonnie Leman (d. 2010), founder and editor of *Quilter's Newsletter Magazine*. The popular *Hands All Around* exhibit is an annual tradition that continues to this day.

1987
George R. Brown Convention Center

First International Quilt Festival to be held at the new George R. Brown Convention Center in downtown Houston. Except for 1991, every subsequent Festival is held at the GRB.

Classic Quilts in Miniature, Quiltmaker Tina Gravatt: Miniature re-creations of notable antique quilts. These minis have been creatively scaled down to doll bed size.

1988

A Decade of Design: A Retrospective of 10 Years of the Fairfield/Concord Fashion Show: A collection of thirty wearable art garments from the previous ten years of runway fashion shows at Festival are displayed.

Quilts: Visions of the World: American debut of an international quilting competition sponsored by *Quilter's Newsletter* at Quilt Expo features forty-one quilts from makers in thirteen countries.

1989

The Quilts of France: 200 Years of Liberté, Egalité, and Fraternité: National quilt guild of France displayed a collection of contemporary French quilts constructed in blue, red, and white as a tribute to France's two hundred years as a republic.

1990

Lone Stars II: Exhibition of quilts discovered during the exhaustive statewide Texas search conducted by Karey Patterson Bresenhan and Nancy O'Bryant Puentes. This exhibition coincided with the publication of their second book on this topic, *Lone Stars II: A Legacy of Texas Quilts, 1936–1986* (Austin: University of Texas Press, 1990).

1991
Astrohall (Festival moved to the Astrohall for this one year only)

Teachers Showcase: Quilts made by some of the eighty instructors for the Festival's quiltmaking academy are exhibited.

Quilters line up for the 1991 Festival at the Astrohall, a Houston exhibit space adjacent to the so-called Eighth Wonder of the World, the Astrodome. Festival was held at the Astrohall only one year.

1992
George R. Brown Convention Center

Festival returns to its permanent home at the George R. Brown Convention Center.

Women in the Eye of the Storm: Quilts reflecting the emotional impact of American and other military involvement in the war against Iraq.

1993

Fourth Quilt Nihon Exhibition—Memories: Twenty-eight award-winning quilts from the authoritative Japanese quilt contest.

1994

Machine Quilting in the '90s: Innovative display of quilts, clothing, soft sculpture, and wall hangings, all created by machine.

1995

Three quilt exhibitions highlighted the great state of Texas: *Rodeo Quilts, Deep in the Heart of Texas*, and *Texas Heritage*.

1996

Sewing Comfort out of Grief: The Oklahoma City Children's Memorial Quilt Exhibition: Quilters expressed their grief by making these quilts in honor of the children and adults who died during the April 19, 1995, attack on the Alfred P. Murrah Federal Building in Oklahoma City.

1997

Quilting a Legacy: Celebrate 50 Years with the Shelburne Museum: Finalists from a competition of new quilts constructed with reproduction fabric from an 1826 quilt. The exhibition honored the fiftieth anniversary of the Shelburne Museum, known for its dedication to preserving quilts.

1998

America Collects Quilts™: Antique quilts from the collection of Byron and Sara Dillow of Nebraska.
Nancy Crow: Constructions included quilts from well-known quiltmaker and artist Nancy Crow.

1999

The Twentieth Century's 100 Best American Quilts: One hundred quilts discovered through the Ultimate Quilt Search with the support of the Alliance for American Quilts, the International Quilt Association, the American Quilt Study Group, and the National Quilting Association. Twenty-four experts from these groups, including Karey and Nancy, volunteered their time to seek and jury quilts. The majority of the hundred outstanding quilts were part of this monumental and historic exhibition at Festival.

2000

International Quilt Festival's Millennium Quilt Contest: A Quilt for the Year 2000: Quilters were invited to make a "quilt for the ages" for this juried competition.

2001

America: From the Heart: Just weeks after the terrorist attacks on 9/11, Festival was remade with an invitation for quilters to submit quilts in response to the tragedy. Over three hundred quilts were submitted, and every one was displayed in a moving and unforgettable exhibition.

2002

A Page from My Book: Journal Quilts 2002—the Journal Quilt Project: Exhibit featured nine small, monthly "quilt pages" from each quilter's personal journals, chosen from 175 participants who utilized personal journaling as a creative exercise.

One quilt on display in another exhibit is ruined by a criminal act. The perpetrator eventually served time in prison.

2003

I Remember Mama: The Hand That Rocked the Cradle: Exhibit featured quilts depicting the artists' memories of their mothers, or the mothers of other people, or motherhood. Variations of this exhibit continued for two more years and were one of the most popular and memorable exhibits at Festival.

2004

Celebrate Great Quilts!: A retrospective of quilting history showcased through traditional quilts from the International Quilt Festival Collection is exhibited for the thirtieth anniversary of Festival.

2005

Best of SAQA: First exhibit of the international organization of SAQA (Studio Art Quilt Associates), the world's largest art quilt group. The exhibition is juried, and the quilts are displayed on special "hard wall" surfaces. SAQA has continued to exhibit annually at Festival.

Hurricane Katrina hit New Orleans, and Quilts Inc. collected thousands of donated quilts under a program called "Quilters Comfort America." In addition, Quilts Inc. organized a fundraising drive that raised $1 million for the Red Cross.

Laura Wasilowski. *Deciduous Decorum*. 2003. 20" × 22" (51 × 56 cm).

This creative quilt was part of the very first exhibition by the Studio Art Quilt Associates at Festival in 2005. SAQA has hosted a major exhibition at Festival annually since then. As SAQA's membership has grown, so too have their exhibitions. The curated exhibitions have a specific theme and size requirements, which gives the entire show a cohesive look. SAQA members submit entries, and hundreds of artists compete for the opportunity to have their quilt chosen by the jurors.

2006

Bernina Fashion Show Daily Showcase: This special exhibit showcased wearable art garments featured in the 2006 Bernina Fashion Show. The displays were changed daily.

America Collects Quilts™*: The Marbaum Collection*: Exhibit of art quilts from the Marbaum Collection, begun twenty-five years earlier, when art quilting was still a novelty.

A wearable art garment by Shari Cole, titled "We Who Rise in the Dawn," was part of the 1997 Bernina Fashion Show.

2007

Quilt of Belonging: First US exhibition of this massive Canadian quilt constructed from 263 blocks featuring motifs from aboriginal / First Nation tribes.

In Full Bloom IV: Floral Quilts in Memory of Helen Pearce O'Bryant: Fourth in a series of juried exhibits of floral quilts celebrating traditional quiltmaking. The exhibition was organized in memory of Helen Pearce O'Bryant, mother of Nancy O'Bryant Puentes and one of the founders of IQA.

2008

The DAR Museum Collection: Quilts from a Young Country: An exhibition of antique quilts from the collection of the Daughters of the American Revolution. This was the first time these quilts had traveled outside the Washington, DC, headquarters of the DAR. The exhibit includes a quilt made by the wife of Francis Scott Key (author of the "Star Spangled Banner").

19th-Century Patchwork Divas: Newly constructed traditional quilts using reproduction fabrics that mimic antique quilts are made by a group of quilters who make and exchange quilt blocks.

2009

Pittsburgh Friendship Quilt: Constructed over many years by volunteers, this quilt is eighty feet wide and consists of thirty-two thousand individual 2¼-inch fabric squares.

Indigos of China: A popular exhibit, educational display, and demonstrations on how to make Chinese indigo.

2010

Art Quilts from the Book 500 Art Quilts: Display featured some of the stunning art quilts featured in the book *500 Art Quilts*, edited by Karey Patterson Bresenhan (New York: Lark Books, 2010). The book sold out in the opening hours of the show.

Baltimore Album Review II: Baltimore's Daughters—Friends Stitch Past to Future: Exhibit of Baltimore Album quilts, either machine made or hand stitched, was popular at the show. Many of the quilts were made by Baltimore Album revivalist Elly Sienkiewicz and her students.

2011

Made in Texas: Lone Star Treasures from the Briscoe Center's Winedale Quilt Collection: Viewing of antique quilts from a prominent Texas collection.

On November 13, Festival founders Karey Patterson Bresenhan and Nancy O'Bryant Puentes celebrate the grand opening of the Texas Quilt Museum (which they founded) in La Grange, Texas.

2012

Susan Lenz: Decision Portraits: Series of fascinating quilts featuring portraits of individuals and highlighting certain decisions they made. One quilt features Karey Patterson Bresenhan and her decision to run and then serve as mayor of her small city, Piney Point Village, which sits within the city limits of Houston.

A New Legacy Revealed: African-American Made Quilts: This collection reflected the genre, technique, and diversity of African American quiltmakers.

Susan Lenz. *Public Servant, Decision Portrait Series*. 2010. Cotton: 25" × 19" (63 × 48 cm). Hand embroidery and beading.

Susan Lenz was thrilled when Karey entrusted her to make a quilt with her portrait for her ongoing portrait series featuring individuals who had made important decisions. Karey sent Susan Lenz the following email, which was the basis of the *Decision* portrait.

"I am an example of a public servant. After organizing my very small city (Piney Point Village, with 1,200 homes) to fight the secret purchase of one of our beautiful homes to be converted to a new City Hall, I agreed to run for Mayor in the next election and serve one term. I won this unpaid position with a big margin and spent the next two years dealing with garbage/recycling issues, flooding, recovery from a massive hurricane that destroyed half our city's trees, starting mobility projects to improve our streets and roads, keeping property taxes stable without increases, reestablishing the concept of open and transparent government, simplifying permitting procedures for new construction or remodeling, hiring a new city administrator, mediating staff disagreements, developing good relations with mayors of neighboring cities to encourage regional cooperation, and so much more. At the same time, I also continued to work as the full-time CEO at my own company, Quilts Inc. Would I do it again? Probably not, now that I know firsthand how much time is involved in being a public servant. Do I regret it? Not for a split second!"

2013

Festival Awareness Project 2013: It's Raining Cats and Dogs: Second installment of a three-year project showcasing quilted pet portraits in a special juried exhibit. Some quilters made fabric postcards and donated them to be sold to benefit a no-kill animal shelter.

2014

Ruby Jubilee: A 40-Year Celebration: Landmark installation of approximately one hundred red-and-white quilts celebrating the royalty of quilts and Festival's fortieth anniversary. The pinnacle was an enormous circular display hung from the ceiling.

2015

What's for Dinner?: Final installment of a three-year display of creatively quilted place mats depicting the makers' favorite foods, dishes, and drinks and displayed on a long dining table.

The Making of Moda: Show highlights included a special exhibition featuring an assortment of quilts from Moda's private collection and educational material showing how fabric is made.

2016

Comfort & Glory: Collections from the Briscoe Center's Winedale Quilt Collection: Quilts made between the 1840s and 2009 from the Winedale Quilt Collection. A new book, *Comfort & Glory* (Austin: University of Texas Press, 2016), by Katherine J. Adams debuted alongside the exhibition.

2017

Water Is Life: Nineteen quilts highlighted the struggles many individuals face with access to clean water and the role women play in rearing families and contributing to society. Exhibition is a collaboration among Quilts for Change, American Exchange in Rome, and the US Mission to the United Nations in Geneva.

2018

In the American Tradition: Recently made quilts that harken back to the time of traditional blocks, styles, and techniques as their design source.

Power of Women: A towering exhibit with many layers celebrating the power of women. Quilters expressed their love and appreciation of an influential mother, sister, aunt, friend, or any greatly admired woman.

Inge Mardal and Steen Hougs. *Pit Stop*. 2004. 65.4" × 65.4" (166 × 166 cm). Whole-cloth painted, machine quilted.

This artistic rendering was awarded First Place in the Two-Person category, sponsored by C&T Publishing, 2004.

The IQA award for Traditional Appliqué in 2017 went to Kathy Wylie of Ontario, Canada, for this stunning quilt titled *For Such a Time as This*.

Sherry Reynolds. *America, Let It Shine*. 86" × 86" (218 × 218 cm).

Sherry made this quilt as a tribute to American values. She incorporated 5,121 Swarovski crystals, one for each word in the original US Constitution, the *Star Spangled Banner*, and the Pledge of Allegiance, and the last 235 crystals represent the years of American independence (as of 2011). The fifty states are represented with a ring of fifty stars. This unforgettable work of art was awarded the 2012 Handi Quilter Best of Show by IQA.

According to the 1994 Quilting in America™ survey, the US was home to approximately fifteen million quilters, who spent approximately $1.6 billion a year on fabric and other related quilting supplies, patterns, books, and machines. Diane Obaldia is pictured here in the center, exhibiting a collection of French fabrics.

This group of industrious women has gathered together to share the quilting duties of this large quilt, working by hand, of course, over a huge, traditional quilt frame. Katrina Ladwig, Ann Arnett, Jane Caldwell, Eloise Thompson, Zelle Letts, and Kathy Smith.

Festival is supported by hundreds of dedicated volunteers. A special set of volunteers, known as the Quilt Angels, are especially skilled at sharing details of the quilt displays. They wear white gloves to protect the art. The Quilt Angel here is showing the back of the quilt to viewers at the 1999 Festival.

Since the first few years of the twenty-first century, International Quilt Festival has attracted approximately sixty thousand visitors each year. Many people visit the special quilt exhibition section of the event, where over 1,600 quilts of all types are on display.

Viewers such as these folks at the 2014 Festival can get an up-close look at the quilts and see construction details and quilt stitches.

Many of the quiltmakers who win the top awards in the IQA competition appear in front of their quilt, talk about how they made it, and answer questions. Linda French is pictured here in front of the quilt she made with Nancy Prince, *On This Winter Day*, which was awarded the Handi Quilter Best of Show Award from the International Quilt Association in 2014.

Maija Brummer. *Mellow Yellow*.
2004. 51" × 51" (129 × 129
cm). Machine quilted.

This brightly colored quilt was
awarded the Runner-Up prize in
the Art Category at 2004
Festival and was on view at the
Husqvarna Viking Gallery of
Quilt Art. The artist shared that
she was inspired by the beauty
of autumn when the leaves are
falling and everything turns
yellow for a short period of
time. *Courtesy of International
Quilt Festival Collection*

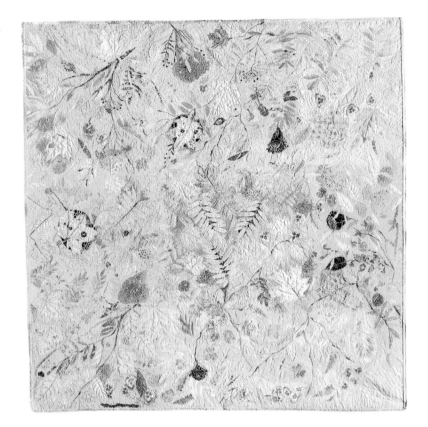

Judith Content. *Tule Fog*. 2007.
79" × 65" (201 × 165 cm).
Arashi shibori dyed, discharged,
silk charmeuse. Machine quilted.

Many of Judith's art quilts
reference Japanese culture, such
as this one in the shape of a
kimono. Her color palette and
abstract nature scenes add a rich
texture to her art. *Courtesy of
International Quilt Festival
Collection*

Jennifer Day. *Garden of Wonder*. 36" × 40" (91 × 102 cm). Machine quilted.

Jennifer is known for a unique type of art whereby her quilts are "thread painted," meaning she achieves incredible clarity and color by covering her base fabric and image with thread via a quilting sewing machine.

Each year, approximately one thousand booths entice shoppers at Festival.

This sweet dog portrait is a detail of an art quilt created by Shannon Conley titled simply *The Dogs*. The dog's name is Bullet, and the quilt was made in 2012 and exhibited at Festival.

In the early days, there were usually two distinct groups of people who attended Festival: those who made quilts, and those who bought quilts. The latter group often included individuals who came to Festival to buy quilts to decorate their homes, or, in some rare cases, they bought quilts to cut up and *wear*!

When Marianne Fons saw this woman wearing a quilted vest and skirt with cowboy boots at the 1985 Festival, she could not resist snapping this photo. For most quilters, cutting up quilts for clothing was an appalling practice, even though many big-name fashion designers, such as Ralph Lauren, were doing just that. Special thanks to Marianne Fons for this photo.

Pat Holly. *Paisley Peacock.* 2009. Cotton, silk fabrics, trims: 72" × 60" (183 × 152 cm). Appliqué, machine quilted.

The Maywood Studio Master Award for Innovative Artistry, 2010.

The design was inspired by an exhibit of Suzani embroideries from Uzbekistan at the Burrell Collection museum outside Glasgow. The quilt-like embroidery designs inspired the borders, and the peacock image was inspired by the idea of a peacock turning into a paisley motif.

Rachel Wetzler. *24/7.* 2004. Cotton: 88" × 88" (234 × 234 cm). Pieced, paper pieced, appliqué, photo transfer, machine quilted.

Awarded First Place, Innovative Pieced, Large, sponsored by Omnigrid, 2005.

This quilt is all about keeping time. At the center is the sun, and the sixty pieces around the sun symbolize sixty seconds in one minute and sixty minutes in one hour. The outermost ring is printed with the twelve months. There are 365 multicolored strips representing the days in a year. Even a leap year is represented— the 365th strip is pieced with two fabrics, one featuring a leap frog.

Helen Pearce O'Bryant (*left*) and Jewel Pearce Patterson (*right*) were sisters who were fiercely close to each other throughout their lives. They are the mothers of Karey Patterson Bresenhan and Nancy O'Bryant Puentes, and the lives of all four women were intimately intertwined with each other and with their shared love of quilts.

Lyric Montgomery Kinard. *The Women of God Know This*. 2005. Hand-dyed cotton: 25" × 48" (63 × 122 cm). Machine quilted.

Part of the special exhibition *I Remember Mama*.

Great Expectations opened in 1974 in Houston. It began as an antique store and quickly morphed into a quilt retail shop. Great Expectations also offered a wide assortment of quilting classes, many taught by Jewel Pearce Patterson and others. One such teacher was Lynn Lewis Young. She is pictured here showing a quilt inside a hoop frame to Dee Ann Teague and Judy Cloninger.

Festival staff member Doris Kosub signs up attendees for classes at the Shamrock Hilton in the early 1980s.

Noriko Endo. *Autumn in Ohio* (top). *Autumn in Ohio II* (bottom).

Japanese artist Noriko Endo creates intricate naturescapes from an extraordinary process she invented where she chops up fabric into tiny pieces and sprinkles the colors on her quilt backing. When the rendition is complete, she covers the fabric in tulle and machine quilts the layers together. *Courtesy of International Quilt Festival Collection*

Jinny Beyer loves using geometry and interlocking patterns to construct her quilts. She created a way to use tessellations to achieve extraordinary patterns and wrote a book for quilters called *Designing Tessellations*. The book was popular in the quilt world, but surprisingly, it also caught the attention of another world altogether—the math world. One day a letter arrived at her home addressed to Dr. Beyer. Her husband was a PhD, so she assumed the letter was for him. He opened the letter and handed it back to her. It was an invitation to speak at an academic event intended for math experts. Jinny accepted the invitation and soon found herself lecturing about quilt construction to a group of mathematicians.

Florence Zentner (d. 2016)
(pictured here holding a
pillow and wearing slippers)
was a fellow quilt shop owner
who encouraged Karey to
begin an industry market.
Photo by Walt Frerck

Arminda Lopez. *Yellow Rose of Texas*. 2013. 74" × 74" (188 × 188 cm). Hand appliquéd, hand quilted.

Some of the blocks in the creative state album quilt are traditional Texas motifs, such as the Alamo and the San Jacinto Monument; other blocks, such as the basket of pecans still on their tree branches, were created by the artist especially for this quilt. *Personal collection of Karey Patterson Bresenhan*

This beautiful Hawaiian-style appliqué quilt titled *Royal Palm* was made by Laverne Mathews, and it holds the distinct honor of being the first quilt to win "Best of Show" by the newly formed International Quilt Association in 1980.

Emily Parson. *Trio*. 2000. 56" × 79" (142 × 201 cm). Machine quilted.

This incredible rendering of butterflies was part of a series of art quilts created by Emily Parson. In 2001, it was awarded the Quilters Only Masters Award for Innovative Artistry. *Courtesy of International Quilt Festival Collection*

Ted Storm-van Weelden.
Nocturnal Garden. 2001.

Won the That Patchwork Place
Best of Show Award in the
International Quilt Association
judged show, 2001.

She spent four years working on
this quilt during a difficult
personal time with several
health issues. Working on this
quilt helped her heal. Some two
hundred *shisha* mirrors are hand
embroidered in this quilt to
reflect her tears. Winning Best
of Show at the 2001 Festival, so
close to 9/11, was especially
meaningful for the artist.

Susan Brubaker Knapp. *Hope Is the Thing*. 2011. Cotton: 48" × 36" (122 × 91 cm). Textile paint, thread paint, machine quilted.

This quilt was part of the 2012 *Dinner at Eight* special exhibition. Susan Brubaker Knapp began working on this piece the morning her mother died, and she says it represents the space between them now that she is gone. One of her mother's favorite poems was written by Emily Dickinson, and the first line is "Hope is the thing with feathers."

Adrienne Lindsay. *Ebb and Flow*.

First Place, Innovative Appliqué, Small, sponsored by EZ Quilting by Wrights, 2005.

Courtesy of International Quilt Festival Collection

Liz Jones. *Hearts and Garlands*.
2007. Cotton: 76" × 76"
(193 × 193 cm). Appliqué,
machine quilted with silk thread.

It was awarded the IQA World
of Beauty Award, sponsored by
eQuilter.com, 2009.

Katherine McKearn and Diane Muse. *Psycho Moms Bake a Cake* (one of a series). Cotton, vintage apron, vintage prints, hand-dyed fabric: 80" × 79". Hand appliqué, rubber stamping.

One of the most popular exhibits of all time was *I Remember Mama*, on view for the 2003, 2004, and 2005 Festivals. Many beautiful and moving quilts were displayed, but the three "Psycho Moms" quilts were truly unforgettable. They stood out for their priceless sense of humor, but also because they were quirky, odd, and memorable.

Sharon Schamber. *Crimson Promises*.

The Maywood Studio Master Award for Innovative Artistry, 2011.

Karey pictured with her Aunt
Helen in the Great Expectations
booth at Festival.

IQA awarded Kathy York its
First Place for *Little Circles*,
2006, in the Art-Abstract, Large
category, which was sponsored
by Hoffman Fabrics.

Pam RuBert. *Towers of Babble*. 2006. Cotton, hand-dyed fabric: 85" × 54". Fused appliqué, machine quilted.

Awarded Second Place, Art, Whimsical, sponsored by Quiltmaker.

The artist included local landmarks from her city, such as a flower shop, a dentist's office, and a polar bear on top of an old-fashioned fur-and-dress shop. The car is fashioned after her first car, a '67 Thunderbird she inherited from her grandmother.

Two Festival goers admiring the quilts on display inside Shamrock Hilton in 1985.

Joan Frantz. *Square Root Cubed*. 2005. 51" × 51" (129 × 129 cm). Machine quilted.

Finalist in the 2005 Husqvarna Viking Gallery of Quilt Art. *Courtesy of International Quilt Festival Collection*

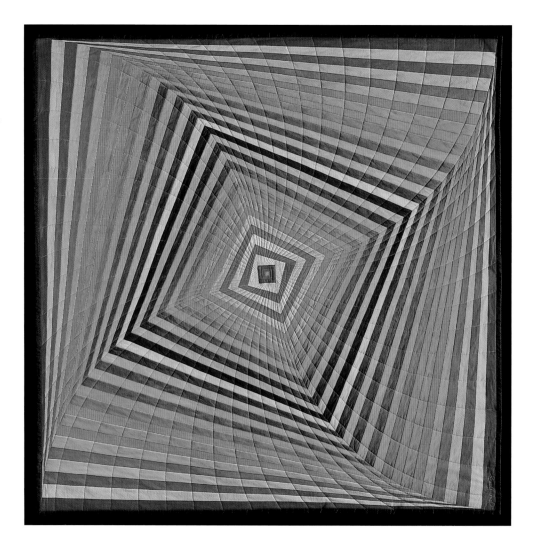

In 1979, Donna Wilder, Priscilla Miller, Anita Wellings, and Karey Patterson Bresenhan developed the groundbreaking Concord-Fairfield Fashion Show, which debuted at Quilt Market, and later Festival, annually before traveling across the country. It continued for many years as the Fairfield Fashion Show (later Bernina Fashion Show).

When the show first began, it was the premier venue for fiber artists to showcase their wearable-art garments. Donna Wilder, who went on to lead FreeSpirit Fabrics, among other successes, said helping create this fashion show was one of her proudest accomplishments.

This photo from the 1980 fashion show at the Shamrock Hotel illustrates the meticulous planning that went into exhibiting both the wearable art and the coordinating trunk show of quilts.

In September 1987, the brand-new George R. Brown Convention Center opened to great fanfare in the spunky city of Houston. The sparkling new facility was humorously coined the Big Ship Quilty Pop (by author Spike Gillespie in her book *Quilty as Charged*) for the center's strange nautical architectural features.

International Quilt Festival has made its home here every year since 1987, except for 1991, when Festival was forced to give up the space and moved to the Astrohall for one year. *Image courtesy of Wikimedia Commons, by Daderot*

Vera Moore poses in front of her quilt titled *Yours Truly Quilt* in 1980.

Deborah Kemball. *Trellis of Red Flowers*. 2008. Cotton: 77" × 70" (195 × 178 cm). Hand appliqué, hand embroidery, hand quilted.

This attractive quilt was awarded the Founders Award, sponsored by International Quilt Festival, 2008.

Margarete Heinisch. *Crown Thy Good with Brotherhood*. 2000.

Karey proudly shows a quilt to US senator from Texas Phil Gramm (*pictured on the left*), June 16, 1986. The other gentlemen pictured was with Texas-based Taylor Bedding, a supplier of quilt batting.

Texas governor Mark White
(served from 1983 to 1987) is
pictured here, along with (*from
left*) Karey, Nancy, Suzanne
Labry, and Kathleen McCrady
in 1985. Both Kathleen and
Suzanne were instrumental in
the effort to prepare the antique
quilts from the Texas Quilt
Search to hang in the state
capitol. The quilt they are
holding was made by Kathleen.

Popular quilter and author
Georgia Bonesteel signs copies
of her books at the 1987
Festival.

The two quilts seen hanging in this 1996 Festival photo were made from the Mountain Mist Sunflower pattern and the Mountain Mist Bed of Peonies pattern. In 1996, Mountain Mist (a batting company) celebrated 150 years of operations.

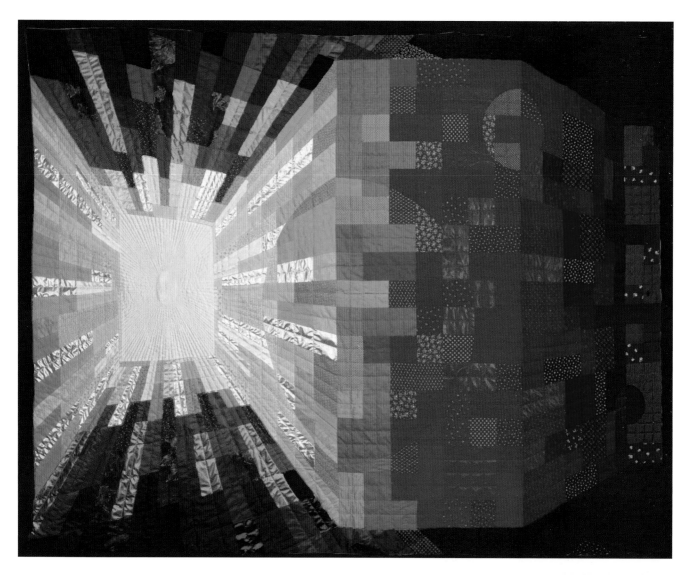

Above: Katie Pasquini Masopust. *Threshold of a Dream*. 1982.

Awarded the Best of Show by the International Quilt Association in 1982, this quilt is considered the first art quilt to win this prestigious award in any large US show. Jinny Beyer was the judge that year, and the choice was significant because art quilting was still in its infancy back in the 1980s.

Left: Quilters at work at the 1984 Festival, held at the Shamrock Hilton.

Right: Appliqué was in vogue for this wearable-art costume at the 1985 Fairfield Fashion Show.

Noriko Masui. *A Mandala of Flowers*. 1997.

This stunning quilt was awarded the That Patchwork Place Best of Show Award by the International Quilt Association in 1997.

Left: Dianne Hire. *Seurat's Dots
and Zydeco.* 65" × 81" (165 ×
206 cm). *Courtesy of
International Quilt Festival
Collection*

Right: This woman pictured at
the 1985 Festival is happily
weighted down in packages
gathered from a day of shopping.

Zena Thorpe. *Kells: Magnum
Opus.* 2001. 90" × 83"
(229 × 211 cm). Hand reverse-
appliqué, hand embroidery,
hand quilted. *Courtesy of
International Quilt Festival
Collection*

Amy Ropple. *Eleanor Ropple* (detail). 2000. Silk, cotton, glass beads, silk flowers: 28" × 31" (71 × 79 cm). Machine quilted.

This memorable portrait is the artist's mother and was based on a photograph taken just one year before she died. It was part of the very popular exhibit *I Remember Mama* on view at the 2003, 2004, and 2005 Festivals. Quilters were invited to submit quilts that depicted memories, joys, dreams, challenges, and sorrows of motherhood.

Judy Coates Perez.
Polychromatic Predilection.
2017. 40" × 40" (102 ×
102 cm).

Part of the *Dinner at Eight*
invitational exhibition at
Festival, 2017.

Ricky Tims. *Songe d'Automne.*
Machine quilted. *Courtesy of
International Quilt Festival
Collection*

Madeline Hawley. *She Can Bake a Cherry Pie*. 2005. Cotton, vinyl, antique handkerchief: 30" × 26" (76 × 66 cm). Appliqué, machine quilted.

Madeline's mother was a pie maker extraordinaire, and she remembers that every family meal had at least two of her luscious pies. Part of the special exhibition *I Remember Mama*, which honored motherhood.

Left: This "Dunk the Directors"—complete with old-timey costumes—seemed like a fun and interesting attraction for the 1991 Festival. There was just one problem. Once Karey got set up in the dunking contraption and someone threw the baseball that dunked her, they realized there was no way for her to get out of the deep, round tank. Someone had to go find a ladder, and then she had to walk through the Festival event in soaking wet clothes. But don't they look spiffy in those cute outfits?

Right: International Quilt Festival at the Astrohall in Houston, next to the famed Astrodome.

The industry has a name for individuals who are wholly absorbed by quilting: Dedicated Quilters. In 2016, there were 16.4 million quilters in the United States, and 12 percent were considered Dedicated Quilters. This special group is overwhelmingly female, on average sixty-four years old, and educated; has been quilting for twenty years; and spends an average of $3,200 per year on her hobby.

An exhibitor at the 1995 Festival offers a demonstration to interested quilters.

Cynthia England. *Piece and Quiet*. 1993. Primarily cottons: 64" × 80" (162 × 203 cm). Machine pieced, machine quilted. Collection of the maker.

This intricate art quilt is based on a photograph and was constructed using thousands of pieces of fabric. It was awarded the International Quilt Association's Best of Show Large in 1993. In addition, *Piece and Quiet* was selected for *Twentieth Century's Best American Quilts* and was exhibited at Festival a second time in 1999.

PART TWO

The Memories

Quilters come to Festival in droves. Some come
in small groups and return with the same group
year after year. This happy group of quilters
attended the 1998 Festival.

Two Women Who Changed the Course of Quilt History

Standing behind the magic show are two of *the* most influential business leaders in the world of quilting. You may not know their names. You may not know their faces. But their story is forever fused with the business they built and the ways they helped create and sustain the entire quilt industry.

Karey Patterson Bresenhan and Nancy O'Bryant Puentes are the two tenacious women who have built and run the International Quilt Festival, plus a whole lot more. The two are cousins who were raised as sisters, and their shared history is a colorful story of five generations of quilters. Their moms, aunts, grandmother, great-grandmother, and even great-great-grandmother made quilts. They literally grew up in, around, and under quilts. A lifelong love affair with quilts led them to an astounding career that took them around the world and revolutionized opportunities in the quilting arts.

Not only did they create their own company, but they created countless opportunities for others, many of whom were women, to start their own companies and small businesses. They helped revive interest in quilting in the US and Europe. Ultimately, their enterprise and the business they own and operate enabled the creation of a total industry that generates just under $4 billion dollars in annual sales in the US.

But it almost never happened.

A Hot Houston August in 1948

A Houston August scalds. August 1948 was no exception. The permeating heat and humidity made its presence known as temperatures reached the upper 90s day after day. That month also happened to be one of the driest months on record in the city's history, making the never-ending heat even more oppressive.

For six-year-old Karey Patterson, that August was unforgettable.

Houston was suffering one of the worst health epidemics in its history: 313 people were struck that year by the debilitating polio virus. Karey was one of them.

Two weeks before Karey was stricken, a young cousin contracted the disease and died. Her extended family was, of course, on high alert. When Karey began showing symptoms her mother, Jewel, immediately took her to the doctor. He informed her that the hospitals were filled to capacity and that Karey would get much better care at home. The doctor prescribed a home regimen that was developed by a nurse in Australia, which called for constant hot packs to be tightly wrapped on the most-affected muscles—in Karey's case, that was her right leg. Jewel and Pat, Karey's young parents, set up a sick bed in the room they dubbed the "cowboy bedroom." The home's previous owners had wallpapered the room with a cowboy motif design, and even though Jewel and Pat had repainted the room yellow, the cowboys still showed through.

From this yellow, cowboy bedroom, in the dog days of summer with no air conditioning anywhere in the house, Karey experienced the true meaning of misery.

Day after day, night after night, boiling strips of wool were wrapped tightly around her leg in an attempt to save her from the ravages of polio. Jewel tore up an old blue bathrobe into thin strips and boiled them on a hot plate she set up next to Karey's bed. She fished out the boiling wool with a part of a wooden broomstick and then used her bare hands to wring out the wool. She wrapped the hot strips around her daughter's leg, repeating this over and over once the wool began to cool. Eventually, Jewel's hands were covered in blisters from the boiling water, but she kept squeezing that scorching wool, praying silently each time that her daughter would recover.

After the initial polio symptoms passed, Karey needed physical therapy in order to learn to walk again. Jewel sought out the best care the city offered. Karey was taken to Houston's primary polio treatment ward, which was located on the tenth floor of the Harris County Jefferson Davis Hospital. Karey has vivid memories of being up in this tall building and looking down over parts of the city she'd never seen before. Jewel eventually transferred Karey to a private facility run by Ed Snapp, a polio victim himself. Snapp led Karey through years of physical therapy, a process she'd repeat many times in her life. His regimen was strict—tough love, one might say. Snapp wanted to prepare his patients as best he could, and he never let them get away with a thing.

With a demanding physical therapy schedule and other treatments, Karey and other school-age children like her were unable to attend regular school. The city of Houston organized the Home Bound Public School Program, and teachers were sent to the homes of polio victims to tutor them during these formative years. Karey was home-schooled through this program for about a year.

By third grade, Karey was ready to return to public school. The Pattersons were informed that Karey would be sent to a special school in downtown Houston where all children with special needs, whether physical or mental, were sent. Jewel immediately balked. She knew this school was not the best option for Karey's education, not to mention the fact that the building was several stories high and had no elevators! Karey could walk, but stairs were out of the question. She approached the school administrators and requested permission for Karey to attend her regular neighborhood school, but there was just one hitch. The school closest to their home also happened to be a multistory building, so she continued fighting.

At the time, Jewel was a talented seamstress who sewed for the public, just as her own mother had done. It just so happened that one of her customers was married to the school district's top physician, and Jewel promptly invited him over to the house. She knew that once he met Karey and saw her walk, her daughter would be allowed to return to a regular school. Karey vividly remembers the day he showed up and asked her to walk across the room. Once he had proof with his own eyes, he agreed to allow Karey to attend Love Elementary, a one-story building.

Years later, Karey's doctors recommended a leg brace to help her young, growing body cope with the disability. Jewel took one look at the heavy, cumbersome brace and said no. Her daughter was not going to be stuck in one of those contraptions. Ironically, some five decades later, difficulties with Karey's leg resurfaced and once again her doctors proposed a leg brace. When Karey saw that brace, she realized that almost nothing had improved since 1948! Like mother, like daughter; Karey refused to wear it. Instead, she and her assistant conducted their own research and were able to find braces used by professional athletes that were modern, light, custom fitted, and effective. Karey wore one of these more modern braces off and on as an adult.

Back in 1948, alongside the misery of that hot August summer, there was another memory that turned out to have a profound and positive impact on Karey. Because there was no air conditioning, the windows were always open. As she lay in her room, confined to her bed, Karey remembers listening to the faraway sounds of drums and bugles, and she was captivated. She learned the music was coming from the practice sessions at the nearby high school from an all-girl drum-and-bugle corps, the Reagan High School Red Coats. As she lay there, enduring painful treatment, Karey made a promise to herself: one day she would walk again, and when she did, she'd march and perform with this group.

Karey eventually attended Reagan High School. She worked hard and had very good grades. Her junior year she qualified to be a member of the Red Coats (that same drum-and-bugle corps she'd heard as a six-year-old). First, she had to audition, which included a test of sorts. Karey was instructed to walk up and down the school hallways twenty times (on crutches, of course) and shout a silly phrase. She complied, even though she was mortified. Oddly, she recalls, no teachers or administrators intervened. Karey conquered the challenge and became a member of the Red Coats. But once she was accepted, a new problem arose.

Karey required a special shoe in order to walk properly. The Red Coats had a full uniform, including matching shoes, but special shoes like Karey's were not available. Karey bought the required shoes and improvised. She used several large rubber bands to hold the shoe on, and then used shoe polish to paint the rubber bands white to match the shoe. It worked, and ultimately Karey blended in with the other Red Coats perfectly, both on and off the marching field. In fact, for the first time Karey felt like she belonged to a group of like-minded girls who were focused on the same things she was: schoolwork and going to college. Many of these friendships have endured over the decades, and looking back on the experience, Karey believes this was her first real opportunity to learn leadership skills.

Identical Cousins

Most every duo has a leader and a follower. One-half sees beyond the horizon while the other's feet are firmly planted on the ground. One-half shines while the other is content to be the "wind beneath my wings," as Bette Midler famously sang. Successful duos share a secret chemistry, and more importantly, a deep sense of trust. The Wright Brothers, Franklin and Eleanor Roosevelt, Bill Gates and Paul Allen. Karey Patterson Bresenhan and Nancy O'Bryant Puentes are one of those duos.

Karey is fascinating, outspoken, and visionary. She is gracious but formidable. Nancy is soft spoken and elegant, with a determined sense of purpose. Outwardly, both exude the ultimate idea of southern charm. While Karey plows toward the future, Nancy softens the edges and fills in the blanks. Together they are the perfect duo.

Karey and Nancy are first cousins who were raised as sisters. They've been by each other's side since birth. Their mothers, Jewel Pearce Patterson and Helen Pearce O'Bryant, were sisters, and the lives of these four women were deeply intertwined. Karey and Nancy collectively refer to Helen and Jewel as "the mothers." The mothers were so close that they shared their own language, a kind of shorthand way of talking to each other that only they could understand. Jewel was the tenacious sister who could do anything, it seemed, from chopping down tree branches to running a business. Had Jewel been born in another era, no doubt she would have had an extraordinary career. Helen was gentle, refined, and steadfast, and she willingly followed and unfailingly supported her older sister, Jewel, throughout her entire life.

Karey and Nancy's relationship shares some similarities. When they went into business together, they decided that Karey, the oldest, would remain the leader. Karey would be the "face" of the company. There was no need to verbalize this decision. It was natural; plain as day. Nancy believes, as novelist Edith Wharton wrote, there are two ways to spread light: one is to be the candle; the other is to be the mirror that reflects it.

However, to say it was a decision made at the time they went into business together is a bit disingenuous, because what actually happened is much more informal. Karey founded the company and is the majority owner. Nancy has helped her with the business since day one, and every day since during the past forty-five years. In fact, during the early years, Nancy had another career and a full-time job, yet she'd always be there to help Karey do whatever needed to be done. Doing so felt natural. That's just what you did in their families.

Both women were career oriented from an early age. Both studied and practiced journalism and public relations. Both were strong writers and excelled at communicating and, much like their mothers, can finish each other's sentences. They can speak volumes to one another without saying a word—just a raised eyebrow or a glance. This relationship is so solid, so evident, that some people refer to them as the "identical cousins."

One of the most enduring qualities they both share is enthusiasm. Not your everyday enthusiasm, but the steadfast kind that shines through day after day, year after year. It never wavers, not even during the toughest times or hardest days.

The Ox Is in the Ditch

The cousins were city girls who grew up in Houston. They did not live in the same house, but looking back, they might as well have.

The family shared an old saying: "If the ox is in the ditch, the whole family has to help get 'em out." For Karey and her immediate family, the ox ended up in the ditch way too often. Her parents, Jewel and Pat, seemed the perfect pair. Jewel was smart and capable. Pat exuded kindness and intelligence. Clearly he was the right man for a strong-willed wife, and Jewel knew it. They were married just six weeks after they met, but it took eight years for Jewel to get pregnant with Karey, and all along she longed for a baby. Karey was born in the tiny East Texas town of Gilmer. Her grandfather wrote in his diary that day that "Pete came, and he was a girl."

When Karey was just six weeks old, Pat and Jewel left the family home and moved with their new baby to the big city of Houston. A few months later, Jewel packed up the baby and headed back to Gilmer to visit with Pat's parents. She took the train to a nearby town, and the family picked them up at the train station. They all piled in the car for the trip back to Gilmer. These were the days long before infant car seats, or even seat belts, so Gran Patterson was holding the baby in the back seat while Jewel was in the front passenger seat. Road construction rerouted them toward a one-lane detour right through a cornfield. They rounded a corner and had a head-on collision with a car coming in the opposite direction. Karey's grandfather was killed instantly. Jewel suffered serious injury to her arm, and Gran was also injured and hospitalized. She had held Karey so close that the baby got a black eye from the button on her grandmother's dress, but otherwise Karey was not injured. Jewel's mother and her sister, Helen, came to Gilmer right away to help out.

The tragic accident was tough on everyone, but especially for Jewel. Her injury was severe. To make matters worse, she ended up falling later and reinjuring herself so badly that she couldn't care for her own baby. Helen took Karey in and cared for her for almost a year while Jewel recovered.

Unfortunately, this would not be the only family tragedy.

When Karey was just eleven years old, her father, Clovis Calvin "Pat" Patterson, was accidentally shot and died instantly. He was only forty-four years old. Now Jewel had a young daughter and no husband. She knew that her part-time job and extra income as a seamstress wouldn't support the two of them. Jewel had attended a two-year community college and had graduated as the class valedictorian, but she knew this wasn't enough. She needed to go back to school and earn a bachelor's degree. At first, she enrolled in night classes, but that seemed to be taking too long. She decided to enroll in all of the remaining classes required for her degree in one summer. In order to survive, she needed help. Helen was there at the ready. Jewel moved in with Helen, and she cooked and cared for Jewel so her sister could focus entirely on school. Karey and Nancy were immediately shipped off to live with one grandmother for six weeks, and then the other grandmother for another six weeks.

As the family saying goes, the ox was really in the ditch at that time.

City Girls with Country Grandmothers

Spending weeks on end with one of their grandmothers was familiar to both girls. It didn't matter if the grandmother was paternal and thus technically a grandmother to only one of the cousins. Karey and Nancy came as a pair, always. Those folks were all family to the girls.

On each visit, an aunt, great-aunt, or grandmother was always sewing, crocheting, or quilting. They made plenty of clothes for the girls, too—matching, of course. Sundresses would be topped off with old-fashioned sun bonnets, and when the girls would traipse around the East Texas neighborhood without their sun-protecting bonnets, at least a half-dozen ladies would call home and report them.

Helen and Jewel's grandmother, Karoline Esmunde Uttech Glaeser, learned to quilt when she was just eight years old. Karey (technically Karoline) is named for her.

Karey and Nancy are cousins who were raised as sisters.

During the 1930s and '40s, it was common for Methodist preachers to rotate from town to town. When a new preacher showed up in Sabinal, Texas, everyone in the church knew that Mrs. Glaeser would make him a quilt as a welcome gift. Quilting was a favorite pastime for all the Glaeser women, and they would often gather together in family quilting bees to stitch the final layers together.

Great-grandmother Karoline gave birth to thirteen children: six girls and seven boys. When her children began having kids of their own, she vowed to make each granddaughter, and even the great-granddaughters, a quilt top that would be given to them before they married.

By the time Karey and Maurice Bresenhan were engaged, Karoline had passed away. One weekend before the wedding, all the women in the family gathered together and quilted the top she had made into a finished wedding quilt. There was no stopping until the task was done. Karey and Nancy were, of course, present and helped stitch those three layers together. They both recall how their Granny Pearce taught them how to make the quilt stitches and warned them to make pretty little stitches because they'd be waking up under a quilt like this for years to come. A few years later, the whole process was repeated when Nancy prepared to marry.

The 1960s: College, Work, Marriage, and More College

For Nancy and Karey, going to college was a given, but paying for it was not so easy. Both girls needed scholarships. For Karey, good grades, notable high school accomplishments, and family hardships helped her earn a four-year scholarship. She finished her bachelor's degree at Sam Houston State University in three years and moved to Austin to start a master's program at the University of Texas. Nancy was attending UT as well, and the two roomed together in a decidedly "ancient" boardinghouse.

In 1963, when Karey and Maurice got married, they moved several times between Austin, Huntsville, and Houston as they finished their degrees and started new jobs. When Nancy graduated from the University of Texas, she remained in Austin and eventually got married and started a career. Nancy had a full-time career outside of quilting in Austin until the mid-1980s, when she joined Karey full time. During that whole period she commuted back and forth to Houston for Festival and a million other work-related days to support Karey.

In 1970, Karey joined the Houston office of Ruder & Finn, a national public-relations agency. She worked her way up the agency ladder and was eventually named a vice president. She was the first woman named VP outside the New York headquarters. Early in 1974, the agency lost a large chunk of business and had to lay off many employees, even closing offices. Karey was one of the ones who lost her job.

The 1970s

Wait, the Women Are Coming?

Both Karey and Nancy were politically savvy. In their early careers, they either worked for elected officials or helped get them elected. When Houston was chosen as the site of the 1973 National Women's Political Caucus (NWPC)—the first such event in over one hundred years—both women jumped at the chance to attend.

True to their entrepreneurial spirit, they did more than just show up. Both women volunteered to help publish a daily newsletter for the convention goers. Each night, they'd gather with other women and hash out the day's news and write articles for what was to come. Sissy Farenthold attended the convention, and being so close to Sissy, whose political experience was epic, was a formative experience for Karey and Nancy. Sissy's name had been offered as a potential vice presidential candidate at the 1972 Democratic National

Karey and Nancy at the 1973 National Women's Political Caucus.

They are pictured here under a poster with photo of Bella Abzug, who was nicknamed "Battling Bella." She was an American lawyer, US representative, social activist, and a well-known leader of the women's movement.

Photos from the 1974 campaign when Karey Patterson Bresenhan ran as a Democrat for the Texas Legislature. Karey was not elected, and later that same year she opened Great Expectations retail store with her mother-in-law, Mary Kelly Bresenhan.

Convention. She had also run for governor of Texas twice, losing both times. Her unabashed feminism and serious political ambitions inspired countless women. The caucus elected Sissy the first national chair of the NWPC.

The event was held at the Rice Hotel, Houston's most posh downtown hotel at the time. The hotel was wrapping up another event as the women were arriving. The men who were attending the first event got wind of the fact that a bunch of women from all over the country were descending on the Rice Hotel to host a political gathering. Some of those men were none too pleased and decided to show their displeasure by deliberately not checking out of their rooms, and sitting in the hotel bar. As the women arrived, they had no rooms to check in to. Many were waiting around the lobby, sitting on their luggage as they waited. Eventually, the women found their momentum and moved past the stubborn men. It was a chaotic beginning.

At some point during the caucus, Karey and Nancy were asked to pose for an event photo underneath a poster featuring a popular icon of the feminist movement, Bella Abzug. That image is now a classic moment from an important era.

Later on, some of these same women formed a local group that supported candidates for office in Houston and Texas, known as the Harris County Women's Political Caucus.

Two Women, One State Office: "Now You Don't Have to Be a Crook"

Karey had considered running for political office while still working at Ruder & Finn. Unemployment, even with its terrors, offered what seemed like a golden opportunity. In 1974, she took it as a sign that this was her time. She filed to run as a Democrat for the Texas State Legislature. Karey believed that the incumbent, Kay Bailey, wasn't doing a good job for Texans. Plus, Kay was a Republican.

Some of the women she worked with in the Houston Women's Political Caucus helped support her campaign. A small number of businesses donated to her, but most of the $40,000 needed to run the campaign came from friends and individuals who believed in her. Some even hosted fundraisers or held art or antique shows. Jewel helped muster volunteers, organized teams to walk the neighborhoods, and, more importantly, kept the office stocked with food! With all that heartfelt help, Karey won the primary.

When it came time for the general election, the opposition put out mailings that encouraged everyone to get out and vote because they were up against a "frighteningly well organized" opponent. Karey was taken aback. No one had ever called her "frighteningly well organized" before. In fact, "organized" was not a word that came up as a descriptor for Karey. Some call her creative, enthusiastic, and even visionary, but rarely organized!

Her opponent, Kay Bailey, had been a cheerleader at the University of Texas and was a former Houston television journalist. Naturally, she had a lot of name recognition. Plus, she was the incumbent. Kay won the election. She later became Kay Bailey Hutchison and served as a US senator from Texas from 1993 to 2013.

At the end of the election day, when the votes were counted and Karey had lost, she made her way through the dwindling crowd of well-wishers to find her mother for comfort.

Jewel put her arms around Karey, hugged her tightly, and told her how happy she was that her daughter "didn't have to go to Austin and be a crook like all the rest of them." Karey was stunned and will remember the moment forever—all that work her mother had done to get her elected, and she didn't even want her to win!

She was at a crossroads and needed a new plan. She had campaign debt, too, which she fully intended to pay back. In those days it was typical to write off political campaign debts, but Karey's debt had come from lots of small donors who knew her, mostly friends and relatives. Karey knew these folks expected to be paid back, and she intended to do so. To help her with this, her mother-in-law offered her the opportunity to open a small antique store. Karey hoped it would be profitable enough to support her half of personal bills and mortgage and eventually provide enough to pay back her debt. It didn't quite work out that way.

Hey Girls, Want a Bank Loan in 1954?
How about 1974? Better Bring a Man Along

Jewel Pearce Patterson had received a $2,500 insurance check after her husband's death. She wanted to combine the check with her savings and a bank loan and apply for a home mortgage. When she showed up at the bank to apply, the banker told her she'd need her husband's signature.

"Well, he's dead," Jewel flatly told him.

The banker tried again. "Then you'll need your father."

"He's dead."

"Your brother?"

"Dead, too."

"Well, Mrs. Patterson, you must have a male signator."

This time Helen couldn't save her sister, but her husband surely could. Hollis Vernon O'Bryant, Nancy's dad, cosigned the mortgage loan with Jewel, and she remained in that house the rest of her life.

That was in 1954, and ironically, exactly twenty years later, Karey would apply for a small business loan and get nearly the very same treatment, in spite of the fact that the United States had just passed the Equal Credit Opportunity Act (1974), which forbid lending institutions from discriminating on the basis of gender or race.

Karey needed the loan to buy her mother-in-law, Mary Kelly Bresenhan, out of the antique store they'd been running jointly. In 1975, they had decided that the family dynamics just made things too tense for them to continue. The two women agreed they would divide the inventory and go their separate ways. When it came time to split the inventory, Mrs. Bresenhan would choose one antique and Karey would quickly choose one that was smaller, or cheaper, or less valuable. Her intent was to give her mother-in-law the best stuff in an attempt to ease the tension, and to show her appreciation for the opportunity to be in business together. This backfired, since Mrs. Bresenhan took offense at the tactic and suggested that Karey just buy her out, fairly sure in the back of her mind that Karey would never have the money to do so.

Karey was determined to find a way. She approached six different banks, and each one told her she'd need her husband's signature. Karey refused all six times because she believed asking Maurice to sign would not only reinforce the banks' continuing discrimination, but it could potentially be a business conflict of interest for her husband.

Finally, nearly at her wit's end and with a chip on her shoulder as big as the Titanic, she walked across the street to the neighborhood Town & Country Bank. This time she tried a new approach. She told them what she needed the loan for, and before the banker could get a word in, Karey offered up front that her husband would not be cosigning the loan, which the bank could not require under the new law. The banker agreed without hesitation—they could sense that Karey was a woman determined to succeed. In fact, the banker told her that people like Karey were just the type of people the bank preferred to grant loans to, because there was no doubt she'd pay it back.

She paid off Mrs. Bresenhan. Finally, Karey was on her own and ready to start running Great Expectations, her own antique store. There was just one problem: after buying out her former partner, she didn't have a lot of inventory. In order to help fill the store with products, Jewel offered her daughter her fabric stash. This wasn't nicely ordered, uncut yardage, but leftovers from her dressmaking business. Karey took the scraps, bagged up them up, and placed them inside a white iron antique baby crib and priced them at thirty-five cents apiece. She hung family quilts around the store to fill the empty spots, Jewel began offering quilting lessons in the store, and Karey was ready for business.

The thirty-five-cent fabric scrap bags sold like candy. The classes filled quickly. Everyone admired the quilts, and many wanted to buy them. From there, history began.

During the early Festival years, attendees were invited to take bus tours to Great Expectations and other local quilt retail stores. These days, Festival goers have several options for day trips, including visits to the Texas Quilt Museum and quilts shops in Galveston, La Grange, Katy, and La Porte.

The interest in quilts got Karey's attention, but she was determined to never sell the family quilts. After a full year in business, she had an idea. There was a midwestern couple, Donna and Bryce Hamilton, who essentially spent their days driving around the country buying and selling old quilts. They'd place an ad in a local newspaper, saying "we buy quilts," and then go to the next town, saying "we sell quilts." Karey offered them an opportunity to sell in her store at a new show—a quilt fair.

They showed up with wonderful quilts. None of them had sleeves (an attachment on the back that makes them easy to hang), and her antique store wasn't geared for hanging so many quilts. Maurice managed to rig up a series of clotheslines down the center of the store and hung the quilts from it with old-fashioned clothespins. Quilts were also hung on the walls and stacked on tables. Karey remembers stepping back once they were done and thinking, wow! She'd never seen that many quilts at one time.

Karey placed a notice in the newspaper announcing the 1975 Quilt Fair at her store, Great Expectations, and invited the public. She considered this fair a way of thanking her current customers, and the community at large, for supporting her during her first year in business. She thought she'd offer them a one-time treat to come and see an exhibition and sale of beautiful quilts. They worked long and hard all night getting everything ready. Nancy was there by her side, of course, along with the mothers, and the family helped during the long hours it took to get everything set up.

Most of the quilts sold on that first Saturday, but there were still a few quilts left for the Sunday crowds. At the end of that Saturday afternoon, however, Bryce Hamilton started pulling quilts off the clothesline and packing up. Karey rushed over to find out what he was doing. He explained that he had a show in Dallas the next week and needed the quilts. Karey quickly told him that that was Dallas's problem, and that these quilts were staying for her show.

The International Quilt Festival was born.

Quilt Festival's Formative Years: 1976, 1977, 1978, and 1979

The 1976 Quilt Fair was held at the quaint yet upscale River Oaks Garden Club Forum of Civics. The Garden Club was built in the 1880s and sits on the edge of Houston's most affluent neighborhood. Karey vividly remembers that a Blue Norther arrived on the first day and changed everything. Anyone who's lived in Texas knows that a Blue Norther can bring a temperature change of thirty degrees or more in just a matter of minutes, not to mention eerie skies, wild wind, and rain. One minute the women waiting to enter (some

of whom had small children and baby strollers) were standing in pleasant sunshine, and the next minute they were being pelted with rain and cold. Yet, they stayed for the fair, and many went home with quilts.

At that show, Karey and her mother, Jewel, cofounded the Quilt Guild of Greater Houston and signed up the first twenty-five members. For the next four years, Karey volunteered to organize annual quilt fairs under the umbrella of the QGGH.

The 1977 Quilt Festival was held at St. Paul's United Methodist Church, a beautiful cathedral located in Houston's museum district. Pepper Cory, who at the time was just a quilter but now is an author, instructor, and fabric designer, remembers attending that early show. She'd traveled from Michigan and stayed with her brother in his dorm room at Rice University. When she arrived at the church parking lot that day, she was dumbfounded by all the interest. Hundreds and hundreds of people showed up, and Pepper was inspired by the sight of that Festival and all those attendees. She was especially awed by Karey, who left a mighty strong impression. She could not afford to return the next year, but she kept her sights on the happenings down south, and before long, in 1981, Pepper loaded her old VW van chock full of antique quilts and fabric and headed to Texas to become a Festival exhibitor.

The 1978 and 1979 Quilt Festivals were held at St. Luke's Methodist Church, inside the cavernous gymnasium. Only a few photos remain, but these quaint images show rows of exhibitors and quilts placed among basketball hoops and seemingly sky-high rafters. In fact, these rafters inside the St. Luke's gym proved to be especially challenging when it came

Four photos survive from the 1978 Quilt Fair inside the gymnasium at St. Luke's Methodist Church in Houston. Attending Festival is an annual ritual, and most quilters attend faithfully year after year.

time to hang quilts. Karey still remembers that task clearly, and she shares a memory that seems funny now but must have been a painful challenge at the time. If she was going to hang quilts, she'd have to figure out how to hang them from the rafters, which would involve her crawling out onto them. She needed help. As she looked around, the only person willing and eager to help her slither out on the rafter was the husband of a quilter—but this man had only one leg. And Karey had only one good leg! True to form, with her optimistic outlook she can laugh at this predicament now. At the time, though, she needed a safer solution, so she called an old boyfriend who owned a set of scaffolding, which was how the quilts got hung in 1978 and 1979.

There were many other priceless moments at those St. Luke's Festivals.

One time they discovered that the overnight security guard, who was assigned to protect the quilts, had left because he'd split his pants wide open. He went home to change and made no other accommodations for security, nor did he even bother to lock the door.

At another point, they saw a woman chasing a man around the parking lot, hitting him with her purse. Hours later they saw this same couple inside, buying fabric. Both of them appeared calm, and he was overheard saying, "Go ahead, honey, buy what you need" and "Are you sure that's enough fabric?" Quilters today might refer to that as *fabric therapy*.

Another day, Karey discovered the quilter who had won the Best of Show award was humbly standing in the long line to enter. Karey proudly took her by the elbow and led her inside to see her quilt and its ribbon. This prize-winning quilter was honored and very clearly moved by the whole event.

One night at Karey's shop, Great Expectations, Karey and Nancy had stayed up late in preparation for the 1979 Quilt Fair. In the wee hours of the morning, when everything was finally set, Nancy was feeling ill and decided to lie down in the store for just a few minutes. She chose what seemed like a comfortable place: the store's window display, which had an actual bed covered with a beautiful quilt. Nancy lay down on the bed and got under the quilt for what she expected to be a few minutes. When she woke up the next morning, people were already busily going about their day outside the store, and some puzzled gawkers were staring right at her.

Later, when the two were unpacking from this same Quilt Fair, the door from the van they were using fell off and hit Karey in the eye. It was Thanksgiving Day, but they managed to find a doctor who agreed to have a look at her. The only problem was that this was the same day as the famous rivalry football game between the University of Texas and Texas A&M. In the doctor's office, both the doctor and Karey's husband, Maurice, had one eye on the football game, and she worried they didn't have any eyes left over for her own!

The excitement and success of these early shows gave every indication that Karey had a future in quilts. After the Quilt Guild of Greater Houston decided not to sponsor any additional Quilt Fairs because they were too labor intensive, Karey decided to get serious and founded Quilts Inc. in 1979. From then on, the Festivals were organized and owned by Quilts Inc., with Karey as president and CEO.

Inventing the Market: The Search for "Yella"

During that same year, 1979, Karey pioneered an entirely new concept. It is the accomplishment that prompts many people to credit Karey with building and enabling the entire quilt industry.

Fellow quilt shop owners saw Karey as a vehicle to help their own businesses, and they encouraged her to keep doing Festival and to do even more. One such colleague, the late Florence Zentner (d. 2016), who owned a quilt store in Minneapolis, used to call Karey "right as rain" every Sunday morning at 9:15. And right as rain, she'd tell Karey she needed to start an industry event. Florence told her, "You can do this, and it'll be good for quilting."

International Quilt Market is a business-to-business trade show conceived, owned, and

Rick Cohan is pictured at the RJR booth at International Quilt Market held at the Albert Thomas Convention Center in Houston, 1986.

organized by Karey. At Market, wholesale exhibitors connect with their customers, retail quilt shop owners. Through Quilts Inc., Karey and Nancy have hosted International Quilt Market in Houston every year since 1979. Market is always scheduled for just a few days before Festival begins. On the basis of the popularity of this event, in 1981 Quilts Inc. began hosting a second event held in the spring in different cities around the US. In addition to an exhibitor floor, the event now also features business seminars, lectures, classes, and other events for quilt industry professionals.

Quilt retail shop owners are pictured here meeting with fabric manufacturers at the 1994 International Quilt Market.

By 1994, at least 75 percent of the fifteen million quilters in the United States are still making quilts by hand, and the Dedicated Quilter would spend approximately $1,300 annually on quilt-related supplies, most of which would be purchased at a local quilt shop.

Margo Krager, Marianne Fons, and Liz Porter at Market (ca. 1993), introducing a new fabric collection featuring 1890s-style reproductions.

In the early 1980s, Marianne Fons and Liz Porter formed what became the successful Fons & Porter partnership. Fons & Porter went on to create *Fons & Porter's Love of Quilting* magazine and a television show on PBS and had other business lines as well.

Most quilters today assume that rotary cutters, oodles of fabric, and fancy machines just naturally evolved. But that didn't simply happen. The industry had to be built: one tool at a time, and one yard of fabric at a time.

Before Quilt Market began, most textiles available for retail sale were intended for garments or home decorating. There were some lines of cotton intended for quilting, but these were not always high quality. What could be found was sold through department stores and chain sewing stores. In fact, for Karey and most quilt shop owners at the time, there wasn't even a decent yellow cotton quilt fabric to be found anywhere. This is the reason she often cheekily says she started Market as a simple search for yellow (or "yella" as Karey tends to pronounce it) fabric, which was in high demand by quilters who wanted to make floral appliqués.

Karey helped change the way exhibitors approached quilting. She brought in fabric manufacturers and taught them about the needs of quilters. She convinced the manufacturers that quilt stores were vibrant businesses and, believe it or not, bought bolts and bolts of fabrics. It's hard to believe in this day and age, but at that time most fabric salesmen just didn't get it—they thought of a quilt shop as being synonymous with a quilter, and assumed they just wanted to buy little bits of fabric here and there. This was not the case, of course, but the manufacturers had to learn.

One exception was Priscilla Miller, a sales director for Concord Fabrics. As a woman in the business world during the 1970s, she was always eager to learn. Karey called her one day and told her she wanted to order bolts of fabric for her quilt shop. Priscilla asked, "What's a quilt shop?" Karey invited her to visit her store, and that trip to Houston turned out to be highly influential in the industry's awakening.

At the next sales meeting after her return to Concord, Priscilla held up her sizable order from Great Expectations and told everyone in the room, "If you are not calling on quilt stores, you're missing a big opportunity."

Concord became one of the first fabric companies to sign up for Market. Once Karey told Fairfield (a batting manufacturer) that Concord had signed up, well, they signed up too. Then other manufacturers wanted in and the list grew. She also brought in patternmakers, publishers, and wholesale notions companies and connected them with quilt store owners. Karey hired a retired business executive from a local outreach educational program and had him come to Market to teach quilt shop owners better ways to run their business.

Market was underway, but with baby steps in the first years, of course. It took several years for these companies and their salesmen to appreciate the mostly women-run quilt businesses and to truly grasp the opportunities they offered. At one early Market, Karey was walking around the morning before the show opening to make sure everything was set. One man had a booth near the front door, and when he saw all the women waiting in line for the Market doors to open, he turned to Karey and asked with disdain, "Who are all those women out there?"

"Sir, those are your *customers*," she sweetly responded.

Nevertheless, after their first experiences, many of those sales reps left Market both stunned and happy, and so did the company owners, the authors, and the pattern companies. They discovered a hungry audience eager to buy their products.

Marianne Fons, cofounder of the highly successful Fons & Porter company, says that without Karey, Bonnie Leman, and Marti Michell, her career in the budding quilting industry would not have been possible. In 1989, Marianne found herself divorced with three young girls to raise on her own. She had already published two quilt books, but without Karey and Quilt Market, she truly believes that success would not have been feasible. She credits Bonnie Leman for creating a national venue for women to join the "party," Marti Michell for giving her and her business partner Liz Porter their first book contract, and Karey specifically for making quilting a legitimate business and sustainable industry.

Historically, trade shows in other industries are organized and run by industry associations or by trade show management companies and often charge membership fees to cover the cost of managing conventions. But Market was started by a quilt shop owner for quilt shop owners, and there is no membership fee to take part in it. In addition, by hosting Market alongside Festival, everyone who attends can view the quilt exhibits set up for Festival. No association or trade show company would have gone to the trouble and expense of installing the top-quality quilt exhibits that Festival did. These exhibits proved to be a priceless educational opportunity for many businesses to keep up with trends in quilting.

Another tactic that set Karey and Nancy's Market apart was the ground rules that were established and tightly maintained. For starters, each exhibitor at Market was required to remain open for business until the very last minute of every day the show was open. No one was allowed to pack up and leave early. They personally understood how difficult it is for a small business owner to get away from their store and make the investment of time and money to attend Market. They determined that if a quilt shop owner could attend only for the last hour of the last day, then she deserved the opportunity to see every exhibitor and all their offerings, not a show that was half closed up. This didn't always sit well with some exhibitors. Over the years, many would complain that they needed to leave early to catch a flight. Karey never wavered. She explained that if exhibitors did not know the rules, then she would read them out loud to remind them. If they could not comply with the rules, they would not be invited back.

One fascinating standard that Karey set early on is part of what helped force the industry awakening quicker than any other tactic. In the beginning, no fabric manufacturer was allowed to sell anything other than 100 percent cotton fabric. No synthetics were allowed. In fact, one year Nancy created a mailer advertising Market as the only trade show offering 100 percent cotton textiles. Karey told each and every fabric manufacturer that if you are not offering fabric that I could sell in my quilt store, then you are not bringing that fabric to Market.

This decision certainly limited the inventory that fabric companies had in stock at the time, and initially there were many complaints. Simultaneously, exhibitors began to realize the Market potential and adapted their products more quickly. This tactic was the very opposite of what a trade association or event management company would have done. It would have been so easy to say, okay, just this once, go ahead and offer your polyester plaids—but Karey wasn't having it. She approached Market as a quilt shop owner. She was advocating for quilters first and was not operating the way a manager trying to fill booths at a trade show would have.

As the industry matured and quilters began experimenting with all sorts of textiles, these rules relaxed. Today's fabric companies offer a wide array of interesting textiles made from unusual materials such as bamboo, cork, or high-tech synthetics.

To help keep Market on track and ahead of the trends, Karey appointed a Market Advisory Council, and in 1983 sixteen women were named to this committee. The council still operates today and is much more diverse as the industry has matured.

Famed art quilter and teacher Yvonne Porcella (d. 2016), knew Karey well back in the early days. While Yvonne was quick to point out that many people deserve credit for furthering the revival in quilting, when it comes to product, tools, and fabric, Karey alone deserves all the credit. She said that almost anyone can put on a nice quilt exhibit, but setting up a trade show for industry is something altogether unique.

Yvonne saw Karey's special blend of toughness and kindness firsthand. Not only did she attend Market and Festival for many years, but she also came to Houston from time to time to teach at Karey's store. Yvonne happened to be in Houston just as Hurricane Alicia hit in 1983. Being from California, she had no idea what to expect. She stopped at a store and bought a six-pack of Perrier water, which turned out to be a silly decision. She also did something else to prepare that was anything but silly: before the storm hit, she walked out of her hotel room, closed her eyes, and fumbled her way along the hallway until she found the stairs. She wanted to remember exactly how she could find the stairs should the hotel lose power and lights. When the hurricane did hit, she felt stuck and alone. Phones were out. She had no idea what to do. Before long, Karey showed up to rescue her. She was aware Karey had problems at her own house, with trees downed, power out, and the need to care both for her mother and her aunt and their homes as well. But Karey made time first to care for Yvonne; after all, Yvonne was her quilt teacher.

Nancy Martin, founder of Martingale / That Patchwork Place, was part of the very first Quilt Market held at the Greenwood Plaza in Houston. She has fond memories of working hard to decorate her booth alongside other exhibitors, and everyone was enthusiastic about this new industry event. In the early years, Nancy said Karey put in considerable effort to arrange fun evening activities such as riverboat rides, gypsy fortune-tellers, and even a Hula-Hoop contest for the exhibitors. Like Marianne Fons, Nancy Martin credits Karey for enabling many people the opportunity to build a career or business in quilting.

While all Markets were memorable, some were particularly challenging. The spring Market in Boston in 1993 was one of those. The dates coincided both with Harvard commencement and the filming of the last episode of the wildly popular TV show *Cheers*. Hotel rooms were scarce. At the convention center host hotel, the hot water ran out repeatedly and guests were sent to the swimming cabana to shower. Hotel management complained that all the guests in the Market room block were showering at the same time, to which the show team agreed, pointing out that they all had somewhere to be at the same time. Other snafus happened in a cascade effect: power went out, stranding a claustrophobic Market executive in an elevator, and problems in the parking garage escalated to the point that a frustrated attendee arrived at the show registration desk and told the registrar to "wipe that grin off your face!" When the frustrated Quilts Inc. staff returned to Houston after the show, the entire registration team quit en masse.

That, however, turned out to be a chance to make lemonade out of lemons. With not much time before fall class enrollment began for Festival and Market, Nancy O'Bryant Puentes's husband, Carlos, a systems analyst, worked long hours to design custom software for computerized class enrollment. With its successful introduction that next fall, the ability to process many more students for classes created new opportunities for growth and expansion. In addition, Carlos's IT savvy also led to the creation of Quilts Inc.'s prototype website, long before many in the industry had one. The company quickly snapped up the very best dot-com domain name of all time: quilts.com.

Nancy Starts Jinny Beyer on the First Quilt Fabric Collection for Quilt Shops

For fabric manufacturers to succeed in selling fabric to quilt shops, they needed the right fabric. And for the quilt shops to succeed, they needed high-quality quilting cotton that differentiated them from the big department stores or chain fabric stores. Karey and Nancy helped solve this problem. In 1980–81, Nancy began working closely with VIP Fabrics, a leading fabric manufacturer at the time. She convinced them to create a collection of quilting cotton that would be distributed only to independent quilt shops. All they needed was to find the right designer.

In the early 1970s, when Jinny Beyer returned to the States from living in India, she had difficulty finding fabrics for the type of quilts she wanted to make. She felt she could design something better, so in 1972 she packed up a portfolio of ideas and quilts and headed off to New York to meet with fabric companies. She secured several meetings, but each time they asked her, "Where did you go to art school? What is your experience in textile design?" They essentially gave her a pat on the head and sent her on her way. It turned out she was about ten years ahead of the real revival.

In 1981, out of the blue she got a call from Nancy O'Bryant Puentes. Nancy explained that she had been working with VIP Fabrics, and the company was eager to create a new collection of quilting cotton. They wanted Jinny (now a famous quilter and teacher) to be the designer. That surprise call set Jinny on a career of fabric design that lasts until this day.

The deal Nancy had arranged was for exclusive distribution to quilt shops, and this suited Jinny just fine. But when the first collection was ready, many of the salesmen complained. The collection had fabric in several colorways, and some of the fabrics were very dark. The salesmen said, "These dark cottons will never sell! We're going to be stuck with all this dark stuff!" The quilt shop owners said, "Oh, thank goodness, we finally have some options with dark prints."

Two years later, VIP Fabrics decided to leave the quilt industry, so Jinny was essentially out of a job as a designer. Almost immediately, Rick Cohan from RJR Fabrics called her and asked Jinny to start designing for them. At first, Jinny declined. Rick dug a little deeper and asked why. She told him the RJR designs were nice, but the quality of their cotton was not up to her standards, and she did not want to put her name on something that was not the very best quality. Rick said, "Well, what if we change the quality?" That was the beginning of a long and gratifying relationship. Jinny now has more than one hundred fabric collections to her credit. She has kept one yard of every fabric she has ever designed. One can only imagine how wonderful this stack of fabric must be!

Looking back, Jinny never had the time to fully appreciate that she was setting new standards. She just did what felt natural and what was good for making quilts. She is quick to give a great deal of credit to Karey and Nancy for making that first collection possible, and for paving the way for other designers to make a living in the quilt industry.

Kindred Spirits in Austin

In 1979, Nancy founded a quilt guild in Austin, Texas, which became the Austin Area Quilt Guild. Two women, Kathleen McCrady and Suzanne Labry, who later became colleagues on another project, attended the first meeting. As charter members, Kathleen and Suzanne, along with several others, were instrumental in ensuring that the new guild would succeed.

To advertise the first meeting, Nancy went around town to grocery stores, laundromats, local restaurants, and other places to hang flyers. She also enlisted the local newspapers, and they ran articles helping to publicize the first meeting. Of course, the family was there by her side, just as she'd been there for them. Helen and Jewel showed up for the first meeting to help get the guild off the ground. In fact, Jewel was the AAQG's first featured speaker. She was a well-known teacher and had taught for years at Great Expectations and many other venues.

Looking back, Kathleen, Suzanne, and Nancy were very proud of that first meeting. Nancy assumed the role as president of the guild for the first year. The next year, Kathleen took over as president and Suzanne served as vice president. Kathleen and Suzanne helped organize annual bus trips for guild members to come to Houston for Festival for many years.

Kathleen celebrated a long and storied career in quilting. She taught, wrote a book, and hosted regular seminars in her backyard on quilt history. Suzanne went on to write the first book on Texas quilt history. In 2009, she began writing columns about traditional quilting styles and quilt history for Quilts Inc.'s website under the title "Suzy's Fancy." Over the years, she has authored over two hundred columns on topics as diverse as Elvis Presley, Barbie, and the Civil War.

Good Housekeeping Great Quilt Contest

America's Bicentennial inspired countless women to take up quilting. Most did it just for the love of making quilts. Some entered local fairs and proudly showed their quilts to the community. In 1976, a huge opportunity came for quilters not only to show their quilts, but also to have the chance to win a grand prize of $2,500, a hefty award for the day. The Great Quilt Contest was sponsored by *Good Housekeeping* magazine, the US Historical Society, and the Museum of American Folk Art. There were 9,954 entries, and Jinny Beyer was one of them.

Jinny had never entered a quilt competition in her life, but in those days she was taking money from her grocery fund and using it to buy fabric for quilts. She thought that it sure would be wonderful to win $2,500 so she could buy more fabric. She set about making a quilt, and at every step she worked very hard to make it her best work. As she packed off the hand-pieced, hand-quilted quilt, she thought "If I don't win, it will be because someone else did better work."

Her quilt *Ray of Light* won the grand prize. Jinny was delighted and deeply honored, and she did use the money to buy more fabric.

The Smithsonian Institution arranged for the quilts to travel the country so everyone could have a chance to see them. In 1980, those quilts made their way to Houston and were shown at the sixth annual Festival.

Jinny Beyer. *Ray of Light*. 1977. Indonesian batiks
and American cottons: 91" × 80" (231 × 203 cm).
Hand pieced, hand quilted. Collection of the maker.

This quilt holds a special place in American
history. It was chosen from approximately ten
thousand entries as first place in the *Good
Housekeeping* / US Historical Society contest for
the Great American Quilt. A collection of these
quilts, including *Ray of Light*, was exhibited at
Festival in 1980.

Judy Murrah

On Monday, December 11, 2017, the quilt world lost a treasure, one who inspired and taught countless quilters over forty-plus years in quilting and sewing. Judy Murrah was as talented as they come. She simply loved quilts and quilters. She loved teaching, she loved her job, she loved Karey and Nancy, and she just loved to share. She shared her story, her skills, and her art. She was endlessly encouraging. Judy was the Vice President of Education and Administration at Quilts Inc., and she will be missed dearly. The countless people she taught and inspired will never forget her. The people whom she encouraged to get involved in teaching at International Quilt Festival will be forever grateful. Her dear friend, Karey Patterson Bresenhan, feels as if she lost a part of herself. She and Judy were together since the beginning, at the store and then the shows. Karey's mother taught Judy how to quilt, but it was Karey who taught Judy how to teach thousands.

Judy Murrah

Here is Judy's story gathered by the author during multiple interviews before she passed away.

For one full week every fall, the huge, semilit hallways and cavernous rooms on the third floor of the George R. Brown Convention Center in Houston turn into what amounts to a junior college for quilters, with hundreds of teachers and thousands of students eager to learn practically everything there is to be taught about the world of quilting at the International Quilt Festival.

The talented executive who channeled this commotion into one tightly organized program each year for more than forty years was Judy Murrah. The numbers say it all: 550 classes, over 150 teachers, and a new record of more than five thousand students in just one week.

Long before Judy became essentially the provost of Quilt Festival university, she herself spent many a day teaching, traveling, and inspiring would-be quilters all over the US. She was one of the longest-serving employees of Quilts Inc., and she clearly remembered the day it all began back in 1976.

Judy was a young wife and mother, and with her one-year-old son in tow, she stopped at a local consignment shop one afternoon and saw someone working on a Sunbonnet Sue appliqué quilt. Judy was intrigued. She struck up a conversation with the woman and soon learned there was a quilt store just down the street. That store was Great Expectations. Judy got back in the car and drove straight there. As is often said, the rest is history. At Great Expectations, she found Karey's mother, Jewel Patterson, teaching classes on how to make quilts, and signed up. She began taking classes with Jewel, and it wasn't long before the student became a teacher.

Judy became famous in the quilt world for her creative quilted jackets, vests, and other garments that feature traditional quilt patterns, and she taught these techniques often. Her first book, *Jacket Jazz* (Woodinville, WA: Martingale, 1993), became a bestseller. Judy originally had no intention of writing a book. It never occurred to her, and she didn't believe she had the skills, the expertise, or the time. She said quite plainly that Karey convinced her to do it. A year later, she published a second book and went on to publish nine in all. Soon, Judy's work teaching and inspiring women became intertwined with Karey's vision to build the quilt industry. She truly believed that without Karey, she would have never accomplished a fraction of what she achieved in her career. Without Karey, Judy might not have even had a career.

Judy's creativity, endless enthusiasm, and tireless dedication not only inspired women to learn to sew and make quilts and clothes, but it empowered a generation of women to feel differently about themselves and what they were capable of accomplishing. So many quilters, teachers, and others will never forget Judy's warm personality, her encouragement, and her countless, yet quiet, accomplishments.

It Takes a Village to Build a City

Running a big show like Festival is akin to running a small city for one week, and every city needs a manager. For Karey and Nancy, that manager was Wilma Hart. Willie, as she's known, was the one who could fix any problem, large or small. For the past forty years, she has loved her job. She even loves doing jobs others would dread. For example, one night the hotel security knocked on Willie's door to inform her she needed to go down to the show floor and help catch rabbits that had escaped from an exhibitor's booth.

Another funny hotel story happened back in the 1980s at the Shamrock Hilton hotel. The Festival attendees who spent the night at the Shamrock were accustomed to an informal atmosphere after hours. They'd often walk around in pajamas and slippers late at night, even to the hotel lobby. At one point, the Shamrock staff sought out Willie and told her to inform the quilters that they needed to be dressed in daytime clothing and should remain in their rooms at night. Willie knew that was a lost cause, and rather than do as asked, she just went to bed.

Another time, it was Willie who had the courage to separate two women fighting who were nearly at the hair-pulling stage over who would be first to enter Market's Sample Spree, a special night of sales with nearly rock-bottom prices.

Willie is often described as a tough cookie, yet one incident nearly moved her to tears. She and others had spent countless hours planning and then hanging a forty-foot quilt from Japan across the ceiling rafters at the convention center. The quilt looked beautiful and could be seen from every angle. But then, the local fire marshal threatened to shut down the entire show because the giant quilt was blocking part of the sprinkler system. Rather than take the quilt down or stop the show, Willie offered another solution: they would plant dozens of extra fire extinguishers on the floor instead. The fire marshal, seeing how her solution would work, agreed to the new plan. The show went on.

Years later, a problem with another exhibit almost created a big void in an out-of-town show. It turned out that one of the planned exhibits somehow never got shipped. Rather than allowing the space to go empty, Willie offered it to an exhibitor at the show. That grateful quilt dealer used her excess inventory to create a special exhibit, and the additional exposure helped her sell a lot of quilts.

Willie was the consummate problem solver for Karey and Nancy. She is currently semiretired and returns to assist with special projects. In the meantime, if a problem arises, Willie still gets the call, and she is still the one who finds that perfect creative solution.

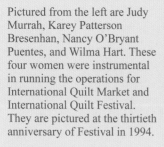

Pictured from the left are Judy Murrah, Karey Patterson Bresenhan, Nancy O'Bryant Puentes, and Wilma Hart. These four women were instrumental in running the operations for International Quilt Market and International Quilt Festival. They are pictured at the thirtieth anniversary of Festival in 1994.

The 1980s

Setting Up Shop in the Shamrock

Compared to some cities, Houston doesn't have a very long history. But what it lacks in longevity it makes up for in "bigness." The history of the Shamrock Hilton hotel is both long and big. It was the biggest hotel constructed in America during the 1940s, and its swimming pool was equally Texas-sized—even large enough for waterskiing shows. The massive 5,000-square-foot lobby was paneled in gorgeous mahogany. For years, famous celebrities stayed there, and many a Houston debutante made her debut in this hallowed venue.

In a passage that certainly signaled a move up to the big time, in 1980 Karey and her newly incorporated Quilts Inc. opened the first of six Festivals inside the Shamrock Hilton. That year, more than six thousand attendees were treated to the largest and most diverse quilt event of its kind, and they came from as far away as France and Japan. The Festival continues to grow, and in 1982, 8,500 people came. The Festival attendees were treated to quilt demos, exhibitions, classes, and seventy-five commercial exhibits featuring thousands of quilts and quilted items for sale.

So many precious stories survive from the Shamrock years that it makes younger quilters long to have been a part of this lore. In those days, the quilt community was small and closely knit. Attendees felt comfortable roaming the Shamrock halls at night in their pajamas, visiting the rooms of other quilters, or even heading down to the lobby in robes and slippers for a cup of coffee, which the Shamrock kept going round the clock. The Houston icon was torn down in 1987.

One larger-than-life quilt tale from this era is the life-sized quilt featuring National Football League star Earl Campbell. Apparently, quilters at Festival in 1980 were so enthralled with this immense depiction of the former University of Texas and Houston Oilers running back that they gathered around him as if that quilt was the *Mona Lisa*.

Quilting was becoming so popular in the 1980s that some quilters evolved to making and wearing quilted garments. This is not to be confused with the trends in which designers such as Ralph Lauren were known to take antique quilts and cut them up to make outfits. Cutting up antique quilts was a practice the quilters abhorred, but making your own items from scratch was a hot new trend. In fact, at the 1982 Festival, author Virginia Avery introduced a new book titled *Quilts to Wear* (New York: Dover, 1982).

In 1985, the word "International" preceded the name "Quilt Festival" for the first time. To reflect the fast-growing global love of quilts, Festival debuted a new international exhibition titled *Hands All Around*, which continues to the present day. This first one included quilts from Australia, Brazil, Canada, Denmark, England, France, Greece, India, Ireland, Japan, New Zealand, Norway, Scotland, South Africa, Switzerland, West Germany, and Tahiti in French Polynesia.

Throughout the 1980s, many quilters who were interviewed felt strongly that Karey was doing much more than merely hosting events. She was in fact bolstering a newfound love of quilts and the quiltmaker. Karey's unwavering love of quilts inspired teachers, quilters, customers, attendees, and even the public to reshape their values to see the quilt and its maker as vital and

In 1980, Gladys Keith made this innovative, almost life-size appliqué quilt featuring noted National Football League player (for the Houston Oilers) Earl Campbell.

The quilt was a commission, and Gladys remembers traveling to multiple quilt stores searching for the exact right shade of light-blue fabric that matched the uniforms of the Houston Oilers. This quilt hung at the 1980 Festival inside the Shamrock Hilton and was quite the showstopper.

Marianne Fons is pictured at the 2006 Festival in front of her quilt *Our Home Sweet Home*.

relevant, and these were fresh ideas at the time. Marianne Fons says that Karey's example helped establish her own values to see the American quilt and its maker as incredibly important contributions to history, particularly women's history.

Marianne was an active member of the nonprofit International Quilt Association, which Karey and Nancy founded with their mothers. It began as the South/ Southwest Quilt Association, before becoming the American International Quilt Association, before becoming the International Quilt Association (IQA). Nancy jokingly says the next iteration will be the Intergalactic Quilt Association.

IQA sponsors an annual Judged Show, which premieres each year at Festival in Houston. Hundreds of quilts compete for nearly $100,000 in cash, nonpurchase prizes in twenty-plus categories. In recent years, more than six hundred quilts are typically entered, and only half of those are juried into the show to be judged.

When Marianne took on the volunteer role as editor of the IQA newsletter back in the 1980s, she remembers getting a personal letter from Karey congratulating her on the quality of her writing. This had a profound impact on Marianne. She was grateful that this industry leader would take time to notice her efforts. As Marianne grew in her career and took on business leadership roles of her own, she had no trouble following the values and examples that Karey had set for the quilt world.

The Mother Patrol

Something that lots of attendees remember is Helen and Jewel standing guard outside the Festival doors at the Shamrock Hilton. Many knew them as "the mothers," so they were dubbed the MPs—the Mother Patrol. Jewel was a stickler about the rules: no badge, no ticket, no entry. Some said they could sneak by Helen from time to time. This ritual of the MPs lasted through many years of Festival, even when they later moved to the George R. Brown Convention Center. In fact, they both volunteered for all of Karey and Nancy's ventures, and the MPs continued their interest in the shows until the end of their lives.

Both Helen and Jewel were extremely talented quilters. In the 1940s and '50s, Jewel ran a business as a seamstress and Helen sometimes helped her with the workload. It seemed that while Helen was capable of very fine stitches, she was less enthusiastic about sewing once she got married. Nancy always remembers being surrounded by quilts, though. Years later, after Nancy moved out, she would go back to visit her mother and find nine or ten quilts piled on her old bed—all of which Helen had bought at Festival. Helen had a special way of making that particular bed. She'd make sure the newest quilts were hidden underneath older ones, and she always placed the same quilt on top. Then, when Nancy's dad would point to the bed and ask if she'd bought *another* new quilt, she'd reply with all honesty, "Why, no! This quilt has been here a long time!"

Karey credits Helen with teaching her the beauty of a well-ordered home. Growing up with Jewel, Karey would always find one creative project or another stacked on just about every available surface in their home. But Helen's house was serene, quiet, and elegant. Nancy adds that her family life was equally tranquil. Her parents loved each other dearly and were always calm and kind. Everyone in the family read a lot, and meals were always cooked to perfection and enjoyed together. Helen never served junk food and made sure Nancy, her brother Hollis, and oftentimes Karey all had nutritious food. Helen was the quintessential homemaker and loved that role.

When Nancy's dad retired and was in the house more often, things changed. Helen went to work for Karey at Great Expectations, even though it was quite a long commute from her home south of Houston. Helen loved being in the store. She was working next to Jewel and Karey, and many times next to Nancy, which was a treat for her. Helen also loved helping customers shop for quilt supplies and choose their favorite fabric colors.

When Karey and Nancy came up with the idea to search the giant state of Texas for its best quilts, the MPs signed on as well. None of the four women fully appreciated at the time how long and how tough the task would prove to be.

Gail Thomas created *The Four Founders* quilt on the basis of a portrait of (*from left*) Karey Patterson Bresenhan, Nancy O'Bryant Puentes, Jewel Pearce Patterson, and Helen O'Bryant. These four women jointly founded the organization that became the International Quilt Association (IQA). *Courtesy of International Quilt Festival Collection.*

Searching for Texas Quilting History

Karey and Nancy have authored three books covering their long search for Texas's most historic and beautiful quilts. The first book was *Lone Stars: A Legacy of Texas Quilts* (Austin: University of Texas Press, 1986; Vol. II, 1990; Vol. III, 2011). Having these books published by University of Texas Press seems like an obvious choice today, but up through the 1980s, UT Press, like most other university publishing companies, had published only scholarly books. Some academics argued that quilts were not scholarly. Karey and Nancy persisted, and eventually their first book was released in 1986. The university affiliation was quite a coup. It also helped open the door for other universities to consider publishing quilt books—the book was popular and sold many copies.

It goes without saying that Texas is a big state. It is precisely 790 miles wide and 660 miles long at the most-distant parts. To travel across it to search for quilts was a massive undertaking, not only in geography but also in time and money. Nancy still had her full-time job at this point, and she and Karey, who was also busy with Festival, traveled from city to city on weekends. Nancy remembers that her personal credit cards were "smoking" from all the expenses. To get the word out, they would send announcements to the local newspaper in

Karey and Nancy have authored three books covering their long search for Texas's most beautiful and historic quilts. To conduct this exhaustive search, the two women initially hosted Quilt Discovery Days in towns across the state. Quilts were documented, photographed, and dated. The first phase of the search culminated in 1986, when they hung dozens of superb quilts in the rotunda of the Texas State Capitol, where this photo was taken. *Photo by Bill Records, Austin, Texas*

advance of the Texas Quilt Discovery Days. Most newspapers gave considerable coverage to this unique happening in their town. Sometimes hundreds of people would show up with their family quilts. Each quilt was documented, photographed, and dated. Many attendees also wanted an appraisal, and time after time Karey and Nancy had to explain that this search was about finding the state's "oldest, best-preserved, most-beautiful quilts," not about how much money they were worth.

At one event, as they were packing up and closing, a young man came rushing in, dressed as if he had just rolled out of bed. He had a panicked look on his face because he'd almost missed the whole thing. He explained that his mom was out of town, and she'd left him strict instructions to get this quilt to the quilt ladies. The quilt he brought turned out to be one of the most treasured quilts of the entire search. It was chosen to be featured in their book, and also as one of the quilts that were hung in the rotunda in the state capitol. When Karey and Nancy saw the young man again, they hardly recognized him in his suit and with his hair combed.

A plethora of stories surround this epic search, which consumed several years of their lives. The MPs helped enormously, and they paid their own way at every step. There were many days when the four women would whisk into a town, set up their materials, prepare for the event, and talk to people all day as they brought in quilts, and at the end of the day they'd take it all down just in time to make a flight to the next town, or back home.

One day, a woman brought in a cherished family quilt, hoping she could sell it. Karey gently explained that they were only documenting the quilts. The woman was terribly disappointed and explained that her sister was sick with cancer and they needed the money. Karey apologized profusely. As the woman turned to leave, Karey, out of the corner of her eye, saw Jewel pick up her purse and discreetly walk over to meet her. The quilt now had a new owner. The woman dried her tears, and Jewel once more proved her kindness and her love of quilts. (The quilt has now been donated to the Briscoe Center for American History at the University of Texas, Austin.)

Karey loved quilts much the same way. Around this same time, she and Maurice were driving down the road and saw a man driving a truck with an outboard motor in the truck bed. Wrapped around the motor was a quilt. Karey asked Maurice to motion the man to pull over, and he did. She gave him twenty bucks and rescued the quilt. It wasn't a masterpiece, but it was a quilt, and for Karey all quilts are worth saving.

Back on the road for the Texas Quilt Discovery Days, one particular flight was unforgettable. Karey and Nancy rushed to the airport after a long, tiring day. They barely made it in time for their flight on a tiny "puddle-jumper" out of Wichita Falls. They schlepped all their bags on the plane, sat down, and sighed a deep breath of relief. Nancy stretched her arms out and let them fall, prepared to relax for the first time all day. Much to her surprise, however, her hand inadvertently ended up in the lap of the passenger behind her. She froze, then heard him lean forward and in his best Texas drawl say, "Well li'l lady, I'll give you two hours to cut that out." Although she laughs at this now, there is still a tiny bit of horror that crosses Nancy's face when she shares the story.

One of their proudest moments came in 1986, when they hung dozens of quilts in the rotunda of the Texas State Capitol. Karey had envisioned this moment throughout the whole search, but even she had doubts it could be done. Nancy's connections in Austin, where she had worked in political circles for many years, proved invaluable. Prior to the unveiling, they wrote a news

Large crowds gathered and the names of quiltmakers formed the "Honor Roll" and were read out loud during the ceremony.

Quilts from Texas Quilt Search are displayed in the rotunda.

release and included the name of every quiltmaker and the year her quilt was made. It was a long list, but some small towns published the entire news release. As a result, many families found the names of relatives through those newspaper articles and came to the capitol for the event. Once they were inside the capitol, much to their surprise, they would find themselves standing next to family members they'd lost touch with or maybe never even knew. This memory, this profound opportunity they created where a few families could reconnect underneath a quilt hanging in the capitol, brings tears to Karey's eye still to this day. Her list of accomplishments is a mile long, but she states that if they put nothing more than "organized the Texas Quilt Search" on her gravestone, that would be fine with her.

Hi Y'all! I'm Lady Bird!

Another short encounter in 1986 left Karey and Nancy with big smiles on their faces.

The pair was given an award called the "Round Top Award" in 1986 in recognition of their work on the quilt search and preserving Texas history through quilting. With the award came the opportunity to display and autograph their books at the popular Round Top antiques fair. They accepted and gladly signed numerous copies of their new *Lone Stars* quilt book. During the antiques fair, their friend the philanthropist Faith Bybee invited Karey and Nancy to stay at her home in Round Top, Texas. When it came time to leave, Faith told them she had just learned that a longtime friend of hers was coming for a visit. Karey and Nancy quickly prepared their exit so they wouldn't interfere, but Faith flatly told them, "You can't leave girls, Lady Bird is coming."

Sure enough, a car swung onto the dirt road, a long trail of dust swirling behind it. In the passenger seat, the former first lady of the United States leaned out the window, gave a big ol' Texas wave, and called out, "Hi y'all! I'm Lady Bird!"

At Faith's insistence, Karey and Nancy presented First Lady Claudia Alta "Lady Bird" Johnson with an autographed copy of *Lone Stars*. The moment seemed both to validate and reward the two for the untold hours and years of unpaid work that had gone into the enormous Texas Quilt Search.

Off to Europe

Classic entrepreneurs share one telltale characteristic: their inability to maintain the status quo. Karey, a classic entrepreneur, is always envisioning what's next. For Karey and Nancy, the next logical step was to expand to Europe.

Looking back, they chuckle about how little they actually knew when they made this decision. They just forged ahead and learned the intricacies of doing business in many different cultures in real time, and they brought others along with them. At first, some of the small quilt businesses that had been founded in the US were reluctant to expand their operations to Europe because they had not done business there before. But many exhibitors followed Karey and Nancy into these new countries, and as a result their business expanded significantly.

This photo was taken to celebrate a job well done at the end of a Quilt Expo in Denmark. The expo was held at a textile museum that had once served as a textile mill, and the museum curators were thrilled at the high number of attendees who attended the Quilt Expo inside their museum.

They hosted the first Quilt Expo Europa (later named Patchwork & Quilt Expo) in 1988 in Salzburg, Austria. For those who took part in this first European event, they hold dear memories and feel proud they were in on the ground floor of a significant expansion for quilting and needle arts. Karey says that to this day, many quilters still come up to her, smile, and simply say, "I was in Salzburg."

The European Expos—which lasted for twenty years—had a clear set of goals. Karey and Nancy wanted to encourage the development of quilting throughout Europe, spread the knowledge about quilting as an art form, build a network of quilters and quilt lovers, introduce the idea of quilts as art to museums and art institutions, and establish more quilt retail stores so quilters could have easy access to products and supplies.

French quilter and author Gül Laporte remembers how alluring the shows that Karey and Nancy brought to Europe were for

From 1988 to 2006, Karey Patterson Bresenhan and Nancy O'Bryant Puentes took the International Quilt Festival and International Quilt Market concept to Europe. In doing so, they helped revive the quilting arts in many European countries. Karey and Nancy are pictured here in Lyon, France, in 1996. *Photo by Pascal Muradian*

quilters. She said that many European textile enthusiasts were enamored with the American dream and the American quilt, and here was a golden opportunity to live the dream, right on their own doorstep.

The International Quilt Association, as a nonprofit, was the perfect sponsor for the European events. As sponsor, IQA was introduced to a large international community of quilters, many of whom became new members, and IQA made lasting connections with local guilds.

Marie Christine Flocard of France, Trix Bühlmann-Epple of Switzerland, and Agnete Staubwasser, a Dane married to a German, along with others who were based in Europe, were instrumental in helping to coordinate these events. Marie Christine and Trix continued working with Karey and Nancy even after the European shows ended.

There were learning experiences and cultural lessons on both sides, around every corner. Karey and Nancy were not always accepted as serious business owners who knew their industry. In preparation for one Expo, they requested ample food and staff on-site for lunch. The management thought this was preposterous because convention attendees (mostly male) typically left the facility to go out for long lunches. These two American women knew quilters weren't going to waste time going out for lunch, and they explained that the quilters would rather eat quickly and have more time to shop and see quilts. The management did not increase food service staff as requested. When the cafeteria staff got overwhelmed by long lines and people waiting for a clean spot to eat, Karey and Nancy, dressed in their business suits and pearls, took dish towels in hand and bused those tables themselves. Doing so was just another part of getting the job done.

Another particularly vivid memory took place in Lyon, France, in 1996. Lyon had just built a new convention center, which was the site for Patchwork & Quilt Expo. The opening ceremony was held at the beautiful opera house in the center of town. When planning the event, everyone had said that traffic in Lyon was light, so getting from the opera house to the Expo would be an easy drive. However, when Karey and Nancy

Just one week before the opening of one of their European shows, Nancy broke four bones in her foot. When she arrived at the hotel, the concierge took pity on her and loaned her a wheelchair. Everyone took turns pushing her, but she declared Judy Murrah her "official pusher" after Judy dislodged the wheelchair from cobblestones and got her to safety just as a large tour bus came barreling down the narrow street. In this photo, Nancy is at the Keukenhof Gardens in Lisse (near The Hague), The Netherlands. The young man pushing her is Mike Calhoun.

left the ceremony, there was a huge traffic jam, and they could not figure out what was going on. They decided to get out and walk. As they got closer, they realized the traffic was due to the immense crowds of people coming to attend Expo! There were lines of buses and cars waiting. Karey and Nancy worked their way to the front and were allowed inside the building. From here, something even more incredible happened.

The women outside the convention center were just dying to get inside and see the quilts. However, because there were so many people (in fact, too-many people), the local fire marshal had locked the facility doors. The women were impatient, and some were furious. They had tickets and they wanted in. Those at the front of the crowd began tapping on the glass front doors with their keys. Soon others joined in. There were so many people tapping on these glass doors that the noise became quite loud. While Karey was trying to negotiate with the fire marshal, the tapping became so powerful that the glass shattered and came thunderously crashing down. Everyone moved quickly, and a large table was placed in front of the doors so people could not enter or be harmed by the broken glass. Karey stood on that table and tried to explain what was going on—in all the craziness, she had forgotten that they could not understand her English. The president of the French guild jumped up on the same table and began explaining in French. Eventually it all got settled. Even though the quilters broke down their brand-new glass doors, in the end the convention center staff thanked Karey and Nancy for revealing a security risk and safety hazard, especially since shortly after Expo, the center hosted a meeting of the G-7 world economic leaders. For the quilt world, this particular Lyon event is now a quilt history legend.

Patchwork & Quilt Expo forever changed the landscape by introducing Europeans to hundreds of important quilt exhibitions and establishing flocks of new dedicated quilters. After experiencing two decades of Patchwork & Quilt Expo, many individuals, quilt groups, and museums rediscovered their own patchwork and quilting roots and have invested time and energy in researching these histories. There are quilt history books that share these traditions in dozens of languages, and countless local websites and social media channels showcase the quilts and quiltmakers of today. European museums have also opened their doors and hearts to quilt exhibitions, and attendees show their appreciation, sometimes with record-breaking attendance.

Host Cities for Patchwork & Quilt Expos
1988: Salzburg, Austria
1990: Odense, Denmark
1992: The Hague, The Netherlands
1994: Karlsruhe, Germany
1996: Lyon, France
1998: Innsbruck, Austria
2000: Strasbourg, France
2002: Barcelona, Spain
2004: The Hague, The Netherlands
2006: Lyon, France

Back to the Future

Jinny Beyer's Festival Lecture on the Future of Quilting—from 1984!

In 1984, Jinny Beyer gave a lecture at International Quilt Festival on the future of quilting. I was dying to know what Jinny had predicted, so in 2018 I called her to see if by chance she remembered that lecture. Not only did she remember it, but she still had her notes!

It's a fascinating forecast, especially for something written thirty-five years ago. But it's much more than just fun reading. For example, what if you took this lecture and replaced the word "contemporary" with "modern"? Would this lecture apply to today's quilt world? You decide. Here's a recap of the original.

Jinny began her lecture by trying to figure out what really sparked the 1970s revival in quilting, and more importantly, why the next decade brought so much angst to the community. It's hard to imagine today, but in the early 1980s machine piecing and machine quilting were avant-garde, and some traditionalists were not too pleased with the new techniques.

She came across a 1984 newspaper article in the *Washington Post* about food and cooking. The point of the article was to show that while many chefs and home cooks were enthralled with making fancy food, sometimes the best food is what Mom made. The reporter was trying to release foodies from the angst of liking macaroni and cheese more than pasta with chèvre-pesto-parsley-walnut sauce. The *Washington Post* was singing the praises of doing your own thing and not being intimidated by what other people were cooking.

That got Jinny to thinking about how this analogy also applied to quilts. For years, quilt recipes were handed down from generation to generation. People made quilts without books and videos showing them how. They just got started and learned as they went.

But then quilting seemed to skip a generation, and many of the quilters who picked it up again in the 1970s were new to the art form. Their grandmothers may have quilted, but perhaps their mothers did not. These newbies used machines! Traditional quilters saw themselves as keepers of the old methods who worked by hand and used only natural-fiber fabrics. They made quilts because they loved them. For the most part, they did not make them as art, and they did not make them to impress anybody. At the same time, they were intimidated by the artsy contemporary quilts, and this created conflict.

Jinny explained that most traditional quilting is actually "contemporary," because contemporary means created in the current time period—so in a sense, everyone is contemporary. The differences arise when you make the quilt and what you do with it.

Traditional quilts were utilitarian. Their most basic purpose was warmth and comfort. The hand-quilting stitches allowed for a product that was soft and flexible, yet still durable. Contemporary quilts, on the other hand, were being made for a variety of purposes, but most were not utilitarian, and the heavy machine quilting left some quilts feeling like cardboard.

Jinny pointed out that some contemporary quilts are being made so fast and furiously that there is a risk they are not artistically pleasing. With the infinite possibilities of machine quilting, it's possible, she warned, that the stitching and the quilt can look like two separate things. At the same time, these quilts were pushing new boundaries and were highly innovative.

This momentum left the traditional quilters feeling guilty. They did not share this drive, and some felt that because they continued making quilts in the same old way, they were not growing. They worried that others would look down upon them for their lack of innovation.

Jinny set the quilters free. She stressed that it's very important for the maker to do what she is most comfortable doing. That was the whole point. God did not drop a bundle of patterns on the quilt world and say, "Here you go, make these forever." Instead, patterns and blocks and styles have evolved and will continue to evolve. So it's okay to be a traditionalist. And it's also okay to be a contemporary maker. Each maker must follow her heart and do what she loves. Sometimes you just want to sew, and it doesn't matter how you go about it. Sometimes you want pot roast and mashed potatoes, and sometimes you want gourmet. The beauty of all this diversity is that in the end, a quilt will be made. And most importantly, she concluded by stating "there will always be a place for traditional quilts."

The 1990s

The Quilters Go to Washington

The plot was thick as mud. Words were flying as fast as fax machines could spit them out. Quilters were outraged and appalled. Both Karey and Nancy made multiple trips to Washington, DC, to try to straighten things out.

On March 21, 1992, those on the side of quilting literally wrapped themselves in quilts as they picketed the National Museum of American History (part of the Smithsonian Institution) and rallied at other points in the nation's capital. Others stayed home but wrote letters. Some twenty-five thousand people signed hundreds of petitions they found circulating at Festival or their local quilt shop. Quilters said the deal was sleazy and downright un-American. Even Al Gore took the side of the quilters. The opposition referred to the brouhaha as "a little caper." Pretty soon this feisty little episode of American history got its own label, The Smithsonian Quilt Controversy.

The Smithsonian Quilt Controversy: Play by Play

Great Expectations, Karey's quilting store, was along Houston's Memorial Drive, a swanky part of town. She was a savvy marketer and was known in the industry both for anticipating and shaping trends. But there was one trend she found very perplexing.

Starting in the early 1990s, sales of finished, handmade quilts made in the US were plummeting at her store and other quilt shops as well. American stores and mail order businesses were readily accepting a flood of cheap, imported quilts, and consumers were buying millions of them. In one example, Jared Block, owner of American Pacific Enterprises, told *Home Furnishings Daily* that his company was importing approximately 100,000 quilts a month into the US from China (*Home Furnishings Daily*, June 1, 1992).

The competition hit retail quilt shops hard.

Especially galling was a set of imported quilts that hit the stores in 1992.

This set of cheap imports had been licensed and commissioned by none other than the Smithsonian Institution. The very entity responsible for the preservation of American history was outsourcing a portion of that history to a factory in China. In 1992, the Smithsonian Institution signed a multiyear licensing agreement with American Pacific Enterprises whereby Chinese workers would reproduce, in mass quantities, some of the museum's most precious antique American quilts.

Karey immediately raised a flag—the American flag. As the owner and president of the only industry trade show, the International Quilt Market, Karey became the voice in this years-long drama for business owners in the industry: three thousand mom and pop (*mostly mom*) quilt shop owners, plus another five hundred or so wholesale fabric companies, patternmakers, notions companies, and others who were making their living in the quilt business. This was a natural role for Karey to assume, but she was definitely not the only voice. Many quilters, quilt guilds, and quilting co-ops took an active role to protest this agreement.

Karey Patterson Bresenhan and Nancy O'Bryant Puentes provided testimony at a March 25, 1993, hearing before the House Appropriations Subcommittee on Interior and Related Agencies.

Four Historic Quilts Lose Their History

The four historic quilts that were licensed were from the quilt treasury of the National Museum of American History, which is part of the Smithsonian. The four quilts were

Bible Quilt, Harriet Powers, 1886
Album Quilt, Eliza Jane Baile, 1850–51
Sunburst Quilt, Anna Sophie Shriver, mid-nineteenth century
Great Seal of the United States, Susan Strong, 1830

The reproduction quilts were for sale through mail order catalogs such as Land's End, Spiegel, and Sundance and were also for sale in major department stores. Each quilt sold for around $150–$250, and initially, each reproduction quilt came with a "certificate" stating it was an authentic Smithsonian reproduction. According to the *Washington Post* (April 10, 1992), during this same time period, the gift shop at the National Museum of American History sold handmade American quilts for $1,150.

The imports irked many quilters, but most especially offensive was the fact that they were labeled as authentic, attempting to convey the idea that buyers were getting a legitimate piece of American history. The quilters argued that the very nature of these reproductions removed the appreciation or consideration of the original quilts and, as a result, stripped them of their history.

Including the Harriet Powers quilt was the final straw for many quilters. Harriet was a freed African American slave who had made a new life for herself. She and her husband were farmers. She had no money yet somehow managed to save bits and pieces of fabric and spent years lovingly crafting a quilt depicting her most cherished scenes from the Bible. The quilt was passed down through a long list of well-documented owners, all of whom today are considered saviors of the quilt. These individuals protected and treasured this precious textile until it landed safely at the Smithsonian.

Quilters were especially angry that the museum had turned this particular quilt over to the Chinese for cheap reproductions. Republican congressman Ralph Regula (Ohio) asked, "How can the Chinese reproduce an American quilt? The answer is they cannot and should not." Democratic senator Al Gore (Tennessee) added his two cents to the debate as well: "There is great irony and insensitivity in the Smithsonian's decision to have Chinese workers reproduce classic American quilts."

While Bonnie Leman, owner and editor of *Quilter's Newsletter Magazine* at the time, helped mobilize the quilters, Karey and Nancy were mobilizing the business owners. They organized petition drives and put together countless fact sheets and documentation to keep everyone informed and on message. They compiled cold, hard facts to demonstrate the loss to American retail businesses: a whopping $46 million in lost revenue the first year alone from this licensing agreement. In 1992, the average retail sale for supplies to make one quilt, including fabric, batting, backing, thread, pattern, and instruction book, was approximately $150. If a store lost two such sales a week, that represented a loss of $300 per week, or over $14,000 per store per year, not to mention the loss of sales of antique or contemporary finished quilts. Karey and Nancy acted quickly to encourage business owners to get involved and write letters, telling them that it may be

In 1992, the Smithsonian Institution signed a multiyear licensing agreement with American Pacific Enterprises whereby Chinese workers were asked to faithfully reproduce, in mass quantities, four of the Smithsonian's most precious American antique quilts.

American quilters were outraged, and a multiyear protest ensued. Karey and Nancy are pictured here reviewing some five hundred petitions that were signed by twenty-five thousand individuals and sent to Washington, DC.

Between the years 1825 and 1840, Susan Strong made a beautiful blue-and-white appliqué quilt titled the *Great Seal*. This historic treasure is part of the permanent collection of the National Museum of American History (part of the Smithsonian Institution).

In 1992, the Smithsonian licensed the reproduction of this quilt and three others to American Pacific Enterprises for reproduction in China. The quilt pictured here is the reproduction quilt made in China. It is 89" × 85" (227 × 216 cm) and is hand appliquéd and hand quilted and sold for about $125. This licensing agreement launched a major protest effort from the American quilt community. Quilters saw these cheap imports as devaluing quilts made in the US.

one of the most important letters they'd ever write. In addition, Karey refused to allow importers of the Smithsonian quilts to participate in the International Quilt Market.

The Smithsonian most definitely heard the uproar, even though they admit it took them completely by surprise. On April 10, 1992, sixteen representatives of the quilt community met with Smithsonian leaders. They were Candy Bell, Jinny Beyer, Karey Patterson Bresenhan, Fred Calland, Viola Canady, Hazel Carter, Lorraine Carter, Judy Elwood, Virginia Gunn, Sue Hannan, Bonnie Leman, Karen O'Dowd, Diann Paarman, Lee Porter, Marie Salazer, and Glenda Shriver. The Smithsonian attendees were Roger Kennedy, director of National Museum of American History, Lisa Stevenson, Spencer Crew, Marilyn Lyons, Linda St. Thomas, and Margaret Gaynor.

Jinny Beyer remembers the meeting well, and she says Karey "was all out for the cause." Some Smithsonian employees came to the meeting clearly irritated. One told Karey, flat out, "You cannot stop us."

Karey smiled and, in her sweet yet seriously determined voice, explained, "Well, we can certainly make it uncomfortable for you, and what's more, we might be able to stop you."

All this drama was big news, and not just in the quilt community. One reporter with the *Washington Post*, Jura Koncius, became intently interested in this story and wrote several articles over a two-year period. There was plenty of other national newspaper and magazine coverage

Harriet Powers. *Bible Quilt.* 1885–1886. Cotton. 75" × 89" (191 × 227 cm). Hand appliqué, hand quilted. Owned by the Smithsonian Institution. Gift of Mr. and Mrs. H. M. Heckman.

This quilt is one of several that were reproduced. Harriet was a freed African American slave who had made a new life for herself; as a result, many quilters were upset the museum had turned this particular quilt over to the Chinese for cheap reproductions. *Image courtesy of Wiki Commons*

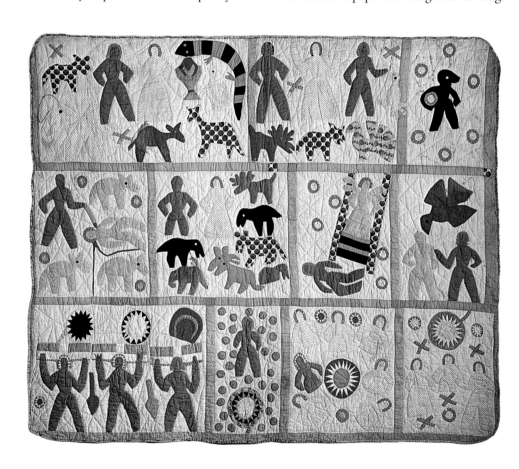

as well, including the *Houston Post*, the *Los Angeles Times*, and *Business Week*. Throughout their careers, Karey and Nancy had done everything in their power to provide journalists with real news, photos, and information. In return, they built relationships with media outlets, and many journalists were very responsive to their calls, especially during this issue.

The Quilters' Requests

The quilting community came to the meeting at the Smithsonian armed with a list of demands. They asked for the following:

1. Rescind the licensing agreement with American Pacific Enterprises.
2. Permanently identify every quilt as an import.
3. Maintain control over advertising and promotional material used to sell the quilts.
4. Attempt to have the remaining quilts made in the US.
5. Verify that only voluntary, paid laborers were working in the Chinese factory (not prisoners, children, or slave labor).
6. If the contract cannot be rescinded, then all proceeds should go to the museum's neglected textile division.

The museum said that the meeting was very healthy and they'd see what they could do. Meanwhile, Karey and Nancy, Bonnie Leman, and everyone else continued encouraging petitions, letters, and faxes. The "fax attacks," as they were called in those days, were particularly effective. Some staff members of elected officials begged the quilters to stop.

Karey and Nancy also went to meet directly with Constance Newman, undersecretary and chief operating officer of the Smithsonian Institution. Meeting with her in person proved to be a powerful moment that helped ensure that the voice of the American quilter was heard. They convinced Constance to meet with the Smithsonian's licensing department, and this concession was considered another victory.

Festival also played an important role. First, Festival goers were offered the chance to sign petitions. Second, they had a chance to actually see the imported quilts for themselves. A special educational exhibition was set up on the show floor, showing a high-quality American-made reproduction quilt alongside a Chinese import. Quilters could get up close and see the stitches, examine the appliqué, and see the difference in fabric quality for themselves.

Next, Karey and Nancy took the required steps to get on the agenda of the House Appropriations Subcommittee on Interior and Related Agencies. This is the committee that oversees the annual budget for the Smithsonian, and the two women were prepared to offer testimony against the Smithsonian Institution's proposed 1994 budget, a majority of which was funded from taxpayer dollars. The hearing was scheduled for March 25, 1993.

But before the two women even arrived in Washington, the Smithsonian had suddenly struck two deals: one with a group of quilters based in Tennessee who were said to be representing the American quilter, and another with a two-hundred-member co-op called Cabin Creek Quilts in West Virginia. The Smithsonian saw these deals as a truce, and they hoped to put the whole ordeal behind them.

The Ladies from Texas are Coming!

When word of these new arrangements got out, the *Washington Post* called Karey for her reaction. "I am extremely surprised, shocked, and dismayed that this has happened. How can the Smithsonian make this agreement with five women from Knoxville? We have been on the agenda of the House Committee for several weeks. I think this is exactly what happened the first time. They think they can get out of this whole mess with signing this little agreement, which has nice goals. But it has so many 'whereas' clauses that there is nothing concrete. Stay tuned for more fireworks. The ladies from Texas are coming" (*Washington Post*, March 25, 1993).

Later that same day, the ladies from Texas braced themselves for their presentation and testimony before the House Appropriations Subcommittee. They were armed with facts but wracked with nerves.

It was a plainspoken taxi driver who set them straight. Just minutes before they walked in the door of the Rayburn House Office Building, he told them, "remember ladies, those congressmen work for you."

The sage advice worked. They smiled at the driver, picked up their fact sheets, grabbed two small quilts they planned to show, and walked inside the government building named for Sam Rayburn (former Speaker of the US House of Representatives, and a fellow Texan). The politically active women from Texas had known for years about the powerful "Mr. Sam," and being in a building named for him was a confidence builder. They'd spent hours preparing, going over their notes, and checking their facts. As they'd been about to leave their Houston office and head to the airport, Karey had run back inside and grabbed two small quilts that would be easy to pack and show. One was a contemporary quilt by Yvonne Porcella, and the other was a traditional Lone Star by Helen Young Frost. Both could be held up as examples made by talented American artisans.

We Brought Quilts!

Kathleen Holland McCrady. *Tribute to the Smithsonian I.* 1995. Cotton: 40" × 40" (102 × 102 cm). Hand quilted.

This quilt was made shortly after the Smithsonian quilt controversy and was constructed using twenty-nine prints from the special RJR fabric collection of reproduction fabrics called "Rising Sun" Collection I. The RJR reproduction fabrics were based on fabrics found in antique quilts from the Smithsonian's collection. Photo taken in 2015 in Austin, Texas.

As soon as they sat down to begin their carefully planned presentation, and before they could utter a word, one of the committee members quickly asked, "Well, what have you ladies brought to show us?"

Karey quickly replied, "Well y'all, we brought quilts!"

This one meeting in particular—the one where they dared to show up and testify against the Smithsonian, an institution larger than life—drew on the strengths Karey and Nancy had been developing their whole careers. Their experience in politics and public relations all came to bear on their approach for this presentation. They had facts, they had twenty-five thousand signatures, they had the unique experience of owning and operating the industry's only trade show, they were authors and founders of quilt-related nonprofits, and they had quilts! They knew this committee of elected officials would eventually see them as qualified and believable.

In the end, the Smithsonian could not cancel their contract with American Pacific Enterprises, but they agreed not to renew it. The quilt world considered this a major victory. The Smithsonian also agreed to stop allowing "certificates" of authenticity to be included with each quilt, and ensured that every quilt would include a label and a permanent marking indicating it was made in China. They also agreed to require American Pacific to have the five remaining quilts on their contract reproduced in the United States.

As for Karey and Nancy, this battle—which they gladly and willingly took on—came at a cost that few people realize. Being the voice for the industry cost money and time. Both women spent thousands of unpaid hours over two years working on this one issue, and all the while they still maintained full-time jobs running Quilts Inc. In addition, they spent a considerable amount of money from their own pockets to cover expenditures for mailing lists, postage, copies, petitions, travel, hotels, quick trips to Washington, and many other expenses. In financial terms, none of these expenses could be recovered. But in intangible terms, all the money and the hours were worth it because the cousins would stop at nothing to save quilts. One quilter explains it this way: Karey knows more than anyone that a rising tide floats all boats.

Through Karey's and Nancy's business contacts established at Quilt Market, they continued their outreach to the Smithsonian and brought the museum many new, revenue-generating ideas that could replace funds from the licensing agreements. The idea was to help the Smithsonian find ways to monetize their quilt collection in a way that would inspire quilters instead of making them angry. One of the primary suggestions was that the Smithsonian should commission a special line of fabrics based on the museum's storied quilt collection. RJR Fabrics was introduced as the company that could make this idea happen.

Other suggestions included developing agreements with companies that produce quilt kits, and agreements with publishers for "how-to" books based on quilts in the museum's collection. Some of those proposals took hold and were successful. For example, RJR Fabrics created a new fabric line called Rising Sun that was inspired by quilts in the Smithsonian collection. The fabric collection featured thirty-nine different fabrics and colorways. Texas quilter, author, and teacher Kathleen McCrady took note. She purchased every fabric in the collection and began making a new quilt she titled *Tribute to the Smithsonian I*. This handmade masterpiece was finished in 1995, and two decades later, when she located this quilt and showed it to the author, she proudly explained that she had used twenty-nine of the RJR fabrics in this one quilt. Kathleen went on to win numerous awards with this quilt, and she was even featured in a multipage article and photo spread in the Land's End Coming Home catalog with this quilt and other quilts she'd made over the years.

At the same time, Land's End also began selling authorized Smithsonian reproduction quilts (which, per the earlier concessions, were made in America). There were fifty to one hundred quilts of each design made by the Cabin Creek Co-op in West Virginia, and they sold for about eight hundred dollars each. This price was an accurate reflection of the commercial value of an American-made quilt at that time.

Beyond the concessions they won from the Smithsonian, there were other good things that came from the whole brouhaha. Two of the quilt leaders in the battle joined forces with two other quilt activists and formed the nonprofit Alliance for American Quilts (now the Quilt Alliance), vowing to work hard to ensure that American quilts were given their proper place in art and in history. The four founders are Karey and Nancy, Eunice Ray, and Shelly Zegart. Furthermore, one outgrowth of the alliance was the establishment of the popular Quilt Index, a single bibliographic source that currently includes over ninety thousand accessible and searchable records—everything from articles, stories, photos, publications, and videos to ephemera related to quilts.

George Bush Sr. Called and He Wants Your Convention Center

As if dealing with the heightened activity around the Smithsonian controversy wasn't enough, just days before the 1992 International Quilt Market began, representatives from the campaign to reelect President George H. W. Bush called Quilts Inc. and spoke to Karey. They wanted her to move out of the George R. Brown Convention Center so they could have the facility for an election night gala (the 1992 Election Day was November 3, which coincided with the opening of Quilt Market).

Karey was shocked that outsiders thought it would be easy to move this international event. She was certain they pictured some simple little exhibition of a few dozen quilts that could just be picked up and moved. Nothing could have been further from the truth. Several thousand people attend Market, and business owners come from some twenty countries. Their livelihood depends on the business they conduct at this trade show.

True to her diplomatic nature, Karey kept her cool and pointed out that Quilts Inc. had contracted for the space years earlier. She politely declined to move the show. When the *Houston Post* called to ask about the status of the request, Karey explained it this way: "It's not a bunch of little old ladies in tennis shoes. These are very sophisticated people. It wasn't that we wanted to be difficult. We're all very patriotic; we're all very good citizens. But we can't move this show. It's not possible." (*Houston Post*, October 1992).

The Twentieth Century Ends

Karey and Nancy Step Up to Make Sure Quilts Are among the "Best of" Lists

Nancy, Karey, and Jewel attend the 1999 Festival together. Seen in the background is part of the spectacular special exhibit of the *Twentieth Century's Best American Quilts*.

The way Karey and Nancy saw it, the twentieth century was simply not going to end without the opportunity to identify the best American quilts. When future generations looked back at the lists of the best movies, books, songs, etc., they needed to see a list of best quilts too. They decided to enlist others and launch a nationwide search to name the one hundred best quilts made in America during the twentieth century.

The Ultimate Quilt Search was launched in May 1999 with the support of the International Quilt Association, the Alliance for American Quilts, the American Quilt Study Group, and the National Quilting Association. Twenty-four experts from these groups, including Karey and Nancy, volunteered their time to seek and judge quilts.

Thousands of quilts were considered, and 1,720 quilts were nominated in the first round. Choosing just a hundred was going to be a painstaking process. Before any of this even happened, all the experts and nonprofits had to be convinced to work together, agree to common goals, and, most importantly, agree on a deadline. It took all of Karey's and Nancy's persuasive powers to convince everyone to work together for this very ambitious goal. For example, prior to one of their conference calls with representatives for all four groups, they created three-ring binders showing the 1,720 nominees and shipped out one for each rep. The binders included full-page color prints of each nominated quilt, along with important information on the final nominees. Presenting the nominations with a full-color photo in a professional style proved that Karey and Nancy were serious about the importance of the project, and ultimately helped coalesce the group.

Seven quilts were chosen by more than half the twenty-four panelists in the first round, and those quilts were automatically named to the final list:

> *Corona II: Solar Eclipse*, Caryl Bryer Fallert-Gentry, 1989
> *Flower Basket Petit Point*, Grace McCance Snyder, 1943
> *Nautical Stars*, Judy Mathieson, 1986
> *Paradise Garden*, Rose Kretsinger, 1945
> *Prosperity Quilt*, Fannie B. Shaw, 1932
> *Ray of Light*, Jinny Beyer, 1977
> *The Matterhorn*, Myrtle Masons Fortner, 1934

Now they just needed to agree on ninety-three more quilts out of the 1,720 nominations. That was a huge task, but eventually the hundred quilts were chosen and everyone was proud of the selections. Now it was time to compile a book and coordinate an exhibition. Again, Karey and Nancy took the lead. They worked with *Quilter's Newsletter Magazine*, which at this point had been acquired by Primedia, to create a book. The final product was more of a magazine than a book, but Karey and Nancy were thrilled to have everything documented. However, there is a funny side story about distributing the book, and it proves once again that people outside the quilt world underestimate the passion, and in this case the sheer number, of dedicated quilters.

Grace McCance Snyder. *Flower Basket Petit Point*. 1942–43. Cotton: 94" × 92" (239 × 234 cm). Hand pieced, hand quilted.

Grace spent sixteen months working on this quilt. It contains 85,875 patches, each of which is a tiny triangle. It takes eight tiny triangles to make one piece about the size of a postage stamp. Grace is a legendary quilter whose life story is preserved in *No Time on My Hands*, a book written down as it was told to her daughter, Nellie Snyder Yost.

This quilt is famous among quilt historians and even in Quilt Festival history. It was shown twice! The first time, it was part of an exhibit at the 1979 show. Nellie flew to the show with this quilt in her personal possession—in fact, a separate seat was purchased just for the quilt. When her plane landed in Dallas for a connecting flight to Houston, an executive of the airline was curious about the seat purchased just for a quilt, so he came to meet the plane and escort Nellie and her quilt to her connecting flight. This quilt was also selected as one of the *Twentieth Century's Best American Quilts* and was exhibited at International Quilt Festival in 1999. *Courtesy of Nebraska State Historical Society, image 828-8.*

The publishers agreed to print ten thousand copies of *The Twentieth Century's Best American Quilts*, edited by Mary Leman Austin (Golden, CO: Primedia, 1999), and Karey and Nancy suggested they ship all ten thousand copies to Houston in order to maximize the prime selling days when the quilts could be seen at Festival. Instead, the publishers decided to ship only two thousand copies, and all two thousand sold on opening night! The publisher had been warned, but it was too difficult for them to fathom this kind of interest and sales. They agreed to rush more copies to Houston right away. The next shipment had only one thousand copies, and those, too, sold out—in fact, quilters were buying them straight out of the shipping boxes.

While the book was popular, it was the exhibition that was superb, and many quilters cherished the opportunity to see these quilts all together. The goal was to display all one hundred quilts, which required quite a bit of finagling, because while most quilts were still in the maker's possession, some were owned by museums, collectors, or companies, and not everyone agreed to loan their quilt for the exhibition. Fortunately, most did.

For the first time, Festival installed a show that would rival a museum's fine-art exhibition. The quilts were hung on hard-surface walls, and the lighting met strict museum standards to avoid light damage. Some of the chosen quilts were on loan from museums, and these institutions had stringent requirements about how they could be displayed. Before Festival opened, museum experts even came to the GRB to test the lighting and approve the displays. Wilma Hart, at that time director of show operations (currently vice president of special projects) and one of Karey's longtime "right hands" at Quilts Inc., managed the whole installation. She and others at the company look back on it as one of their finest shows.

Roberta Horton, a well-known quilter and teacher, remembers being blown away by the exhibit. She'd seen photos of some of the quilts and had heard about some of the others, but to see them all together, right there in Houston, was astounding. As Karey and Nancy watched Roberta and others take it all in, they frequently saw tears of joy. For quilt lovers, this was heaven.

Terrie Hancock Mangat. *Dashboard Saints: In Memory of St. Christopher (Who Lost His Magnetism)*. 1985. Cotton: 99" × 124" (251 × 315 cm). Transfer print, hand appliqué, reverse appliqué, embroidery, machine quilted.

This creative art quilt was selected for inclusion in the *Twentieth Century's Best American Quilts* and was exhibited at Festival in 1999. *Courtesy of International Quilt Study Center & Museum, University of Nebraska-Lincoln, 1997.007.1093, www. QuiltStudy.org*

2000–2009

Working through the 9/11 Tragedy

The 9/11 terrorist attacks took place only six weeks before the 2001 Festival. *America: From the Heart* included more than three hundred quilts that were sent in from all over the world. This powerful exhibition was a remarkable, emotional collection, and many Festival attendees have very strong memories of seeing these quilts.

The day after terrorists attacked American soil, Karey gathered her small staff together for a meeting. They cried. They prayed. They sang. And they vowed to remake Festival to honor this tragedy. Festival—an event that takes the better part of a year to plan—was only six weeks away, but no one in that meeting doubted they could do it.

The first order of business was for Karey to inform her staff that if anyone wanted to cancel—it didn't matter if they were an exhibitor, teacher, or attendee—they could do so with a full refund. The staff worried. What if everyone canceled? Karey and Nancy reassured everyone they would do whatever it took to accommodate quilters in this crisis. Karey wrote in the annual Festival program that "What we have to do now is live our lives. Love one another. Treasure our liberty. Support our country. Honor our values. Make our quilts. And keep going." Deep down, she knew quilters would keep going.

Karey and Nancy wanted to remake the exhibits to allow quilters to express themselves in the way they do best: making quilts. They put out word that anyone who had made or wanted to make a patriotic quilt or a quilt in response to the tragedy could send it to Festival. The exhibit *America: From the Heart* was an open exhibition—no juries, no size restrictions. Karey anticipated that with just six weeks to go, they would receive about fifty or so quilts. Instead, they

got over three hundred, and they came from all over the world. Many quilters remember going to work on their quilts immediately, and some recall staying up all night. Quilts were still arriving at the convention center as the show was starting.

Caryl Bryer Fallert-Gentry, a former flight attendant, made a quilt for the exhibit and knew that if anyone could remake Festival in this short time period, Karey could do it. Caryl had always admired Karey's fortitude and professionalism, and she was certain when she got to Houston that this Festival would not disappoint.

She was right. Every quilt was hung, and the result was incredibly moving and dramatic. The "Main Street" of the giant exhibitor hall was completely remade. In the aisle spaces where one would normally find quilt displays and demos for new tools and gadgets, these intensely emotional quilts were hung along the red carpet underneath a giant American flag. Living through this unsure time was surreal and frightening, but seeing these quilts was uplifting. Tissue boxes were stationed along the exhibit for teary eyes.

Before 9/11, Marianne Webb had made a powerful quilt that included the words of the song "God Bless the USA" (written and performed by Lee Greenwood) stitched over the white fabric stripes of an American flag design. This quilt seemed the obvious choice for the Festival's program cover, but they'd need permission to publish the quilt's image due to the song's copyright. Not only did Nancy's Publications and Public Information staff ditch the previous program, but they managed to obtain permission to publish Marianne's quilt and completely redesigned the Festival and Market programs in time for opening night.

Quilters whose work was featured in *America: From the Heart* were given the opportunity to donate those quilts to an auction to raise funds for the Families of Freedom Scholarship

Caryl Bryer Fallert-Gentry. *Response #1: Stunned.* 2001.

Exhibited in *America: From the Heart* at the 2001 Festival.

Making this quilt was very personal for Caryl. Up until the late 1990s, she worked as a flight attendant for American Airlines. When four planes went down on September 11, Caryl could picture what was happening inside those planes and how the crew would try to respond. She was never one to make art about negative subjects, but she felt compelled to create this one. The quilt is simultaneously stark, colorful, and incredibly powerful.

Spirit of America was made by Christy Johnson and exhibited in *America: From the Heart*.

Fund (which was created to provide education for the victims or their survivors). As the auction was underway, two bidders were bidding against each other on the same quilt. Karey was one of the bidders, and it was a quilt she really wanted for her personal collection. The other bidder, who stood just a foot away from Karey, worked for American Airlines. She had tears in her eyes just looking at that quilt. She had no idea who Karey was, nor did she know Karey was the one bidding against her. As they talked, she shared how much she wanted to win that quilt. Karey assured her, "Don't worry, I'm sure you'll win it." And she did.

Not only did individuals bid on the quilts, but most of the companies exhibiting and participating at Market and Festival also made generous donations to the charity. C&T Publishing agreed to publish a book of the quilts, also called *America: From the Heart*, and to donate all profits to the Families of Freedom Scholarship Fund. Karey and Nancy are proud of what they and everyone on the staff accomplished in such a short time, and especially the causes they supported.

Jinny Beyer. *Windows*. Cotton: 2002. Hand pieced, hand quilted, made in response to 9/11.

She began the quilt shortly after the attacks, and the last stitch was taken on October 5, 2002. This quilt was exhibited with the *America: From the Heart* exhibition when it traveled after the initial viewing in Houston. The faded reds, whites, and blues represent colors that could have been tinged with smoke and ash, while the occasional vibrant tone represents strength and courage. The title reflects all the windows that came to mind during this tragedy, such as those in airplanes, the World Trade Center, emergency vehicles, and even the stained-glass windows of Jinny's local church, where strangers gathered to hold hands and pray. The quilt contains 4,777 pieces of fabric. The center piece is for Jinny's neighbor and friend, Barbara Olson, who was in the plane that hit the Pentagon.

Susan Shie. *Liberty Weeps for Her Country*. White cotton: 44" × 34" (112 × 86 cm). Began construction September 13, 2001. Finished September 19, 2001. Whole-cloth airbrushed and painted art quilt. Embellished with glass beads, polymer clay faces made by the artist, buttons, antique clothespins, sequined snake appliqués, ceramic alphabet beads, etc. Machine quilted.

Exhibited in *America: From the Heart*.

Main Street of the giant exhibit hall was completely remade for the 9/11 exhibit *America: From the Heart*.

Silver Star Award Winners

The Silver Star Award program was created by Karey and Nancy as a way of recognizing living persons who have made a lasting and positive impact on the field of quilting and textile art:

1994: Bonnie Leman	2002: Nancy Martin
1995: Jinny Beyer	2003: Elly Sienkiewicz
1996: Virginia Avery	2004: Marti Michell
1997: Jean Ray Laury	2005: Katie Pasquini Masopust
1998: Yvonne Porcella	2006: Caryl Bryer Fallert-Gentry
1999: Donna Wilder	2007: Michael James
2000: Roberta Horton	2008: Alex Anderson
2001: Georgia Bonesteel	

Yvonne Porcella: "When I won I was so proud. I wanted to give something back to Karey to thank her for the recognition, so I had a special pin made for her and sent it to her."

Roberta Horton: "I got a letter telling me I had won the Silver Star. I was so overwhelmed at being chosen that I didn't even think to write a letter back. Karey finally called me personally to see if I would accept the award. It was such a wonderful validation and said to me that what I was doing was okay."

Katie Pasquini Masopust: "Winning this award was pretty awesome. My whole family entourage came to the event. It was a wonderful memory that seemed to last an entire week. I felt like I was walking on air. When my family and I were at the awards event, I could see my brother walking up to Karey and I was mortified, having no idea what he would say to the woman we all revered. He asked Karey: 'What do you attribute all your success to?' And without skipping a beat, she said 'fresh flowers.'"

Caryl Bryer Fallert-Gentry: "Being named the Silver Star is the biggest honor I will ever get in my life."

Alex Anderson: "I have had the delicious honor of ushering many new quilters into 'the fold' through various means of communication: the printed page, television, and now through the astonishing educational and communicative aspects of the internet. To receive the Silver Star Award on behalf of these efforts is a huge and unexpected honor."

Elly Sienkiewicz: "All through the decades of International Quilt Festival, I've lived in our nation's capital, Washington, DC. So, dining at local restaurants, my first Quilt Festival amidst strolling mariachis was so thrillingly 'Texas!' for me. Years passed, then, in 2003, Ms. Karey B. came to DC for business. She invited me to join her and Judy Murrah for dinner, where she shared that I was to be honored with the 2003 Silver Star Award. A celebratory dinner would be held during the International Quilt Festival, she informed me, and I was to give a presentation thirty minutes long—an intense, dark-eyed-beauty glance told me this time limit was firm. I was to provide a retrospective of my work. At Festival, I was so very happy. Karey presented what has become a cherished Sienkiewicz family heirloom, a custom silversmith-designed brooch. At the elegant Silver Star dinner, I was to give my presentation, which I had worked on for months. That speech began, 'Tonight, I'll talk about gifts: how I got here and who I have to thank for it, the gifts of appliqué and Album Quilts, and what our own gifts may give the future.'"

Jewel Pearce Patterson Scholarship Award

Named in honor of Karey's mother, who taught countless people how to quilt, the Jewel Pearce Patterson Scholarship Award for Quilting Teachers recognizes quilters who teach, and is intended to support and expand their teaching career. Originally, the award was intended to bring European teachers to Festival in the US, and to take US teachers to Patchwork and Quilt Expo in Europe. After Karey and Nancy ended Expo, the award no longer had that restriction, and it was given to the best applicant that year.

When Lisa Walton, recipient of the 2010 award, learned she had won, she screamed in delight. Unfortunately, she was reading her email in the car while her husband was driving, and the scream nearly sent him off the road! She was in disbelief. "Here is little me . . . far away in Australia, and bloody hell, this was just astounding recognition."

Lisa credits this award for significantly boosting her confidence in the quilt world. When she came to Houston for the awards ceremony, Karey walked up on stage and said, "Is Lisa Walton in the audience?" Lisa was in shock. She was sitting behind all "these famous quilters," yet for this one day she got to sit at the "bride's table" and was introduced at several events. Years later, Lisa met Karey again at Festival and thanked her profusely for changing her life. She recalls that Karey smiled sweetly and said, "Thank *you*."

Pam Holland. *Ode to Jewel Pearce Patterson: A Gift to Karey Patterson Bresenhan*. 2014. Cotton: 40" × 40" (102 × 102 cm). Thread painted, raw-edge machine appliquéd, machine quilted.

In 2000, Pam Holland won the Jewel Pearce Patterson Scholarship for Quilting Teachers, and she credits this important recognition for changing her quilting life. Pam, who lives in Australia, has traveled the world as a quilt teacher, artist, blogger, and photographer. *Courtesy of International Quilt Festival Collection*

1991: Shelly Burge, Nebraska
1992: Lynne Edwards, England
1993: Cindy Blackberg, Florida
1993: Dianne Finnegan, Australia
1994: Brenda Groelz, Nebraska
1997: Anna Dolanyi, Hungary
1998: Bonnie Lyn McCaffery, Pennsylvania
1999: Janice Gunner, England
2000: Pam Holland, Australia

2002: Pepper Cory, North Carolina
2003: Donna Ward, New Zealand
2004: Jenny Raymond, Nebraska
2006: Jackie Robinson, Missouri
2007: Tricia Quirk Spitzmueller, Minnesota
2008: Kathy Kansier, Missouri
2009: Wendy Butler Berns, Wisconsin
2010: Lisa Walton, Australia

Quilt Trivia

The following excerpts were written by Suzanne Labry for the International Quilt Festival newsletter and website. Her column is called "Suzy's Fancy."

Quilts Tell Stories—If Only We Take Time to Read Them!

In a mystery play written in 1916 by Susan Glaspell, two women accompany the sheriff and county attorney to a farmhouse where a man has been murdered. The women are there to gather some clothing to take to the dead man's wife, who has been arrested as the prime suspect.

The men are trying to discover evidence to support the murder charge but can find nothing. The women, however, quickly figure out that the wife is indeed guilty, and they do so partially by looking at the quilt that she was making prior to her husband's death. They can tell from the Log Cabin blocks she was working on that something caused her to snap—the workmanship that had been consistently neat and precise suddenly had become wildly irregular in the block where the wife's needle remained.

The use of a quilt as a secret code that is recognized and understood only by women is crucial to the resolution of Glaspell's story. It represents something distinctly female: both an item and an activity flying under the radar of male detection or interest. While social mores have changed more than a century onward, the tale still has the power to make us think about the way that society views women's work. It also reminds us that quilts tell stories—if only we take time to read them!

A Willie Nelson Woodstock in the Texas Mud in 1976 Yields a Quilt Collection

In 1976, the historic south-central Texas town of Gonzales was home to the Willie Nelson Fourth of July picnic—eighty-five thousand concertgoers descended upon the small town, and torrential rains turned the rural event site into an enormous mud pit.

The next morning, as bedraggled concertgoers left the scene, John Dromgoole and his friends decided to wait until the crowd thinned and traffic lessened before leaving themselves. While walking around the ruined pasture, Dromgoole kept noticing pieces of fabric protruding from the mud. Finally, he stopped and tugged on one of the pieces, and to this surprise, he realized that it was a quilt—intended as a spot to sit on during the concert—that had been trampled into the mud and left behind by its owner.

Wherever he saw a bit of quilt sticking up, Dromgoole extracted it from the mud and dragged it over to the van that he and his friends had come in. By the time he finished, he had recovered close to twenty quilts.

Dromgoole somehow managed to load the sodden, mud-caked quilts into the van, and upon arriving home, he first hosed them down outside, then took them to a commercial laundry and washed them numerous times. Cleansed of their mud coating, the quilts revealed themselves, surprisingly intact.

"These were somebody's heirlooms, something a grandmother or mother had made." Dromgoole's "collection" just goes to show that you never know when, where, and how quilts might become a part of your life—even when least expected.

What the Heck Are Chicken Linens?

"Feed sacks" are most commonly associated with the Great Depression or earlier . . . but it may surprise some to know that the printed textile bags were still commonly used in rural areas during the 1950s and 1960s. My aunt selected her "staples" not by their brand name but rather by the fabric bag they came in.

In a 1946 *Time* magazine article titled "Women: Foul Rumor," a manager from Pillsbury Flour was quoted as saying, "They used to say that when the wind blew across the South you could see our trade name on all the girls' underpants."

As paper began to replace cotton in the bag-manufacturing industry in the 1950s, the National Cotton Council partnered with the Textile Bag Manufacturers Association in an attempt to slow that crossover by sponsoring the Cotton Bag Sewing Queen Contest.

The contest was held at state fairs nationwide throughout the 1950s and 1960s, and participants were encouraged to "Buy your commodities in cotton—sew the bags to win cash, sewing machines, home appliances and other valuable gifts including a Free Vacation in Hollywood! A full week of exciting and glamorous entertaining in Southern California awaits the 1960 Cotton Bag Sewing Queen and her first alternate. Each may bring a companion of her choosing and select her mode of transportation—by jet, if available!" (Smithsonian).

My Aunt Neva never entered a Cotton Bag Sewing Queen Contest. I doubt if my (or my brother's!) bonnet stiffened with "slats" of cardboard from a Big Chief writing tablet would have made the cut in any case. Nevertheless, she and many women like her made use of every scrap of the fabric that came her way via a sack of chicken feed or a bag of flour.

The 2010s

Red and White Quilts as Far as the Eye Can See

"I feel like I've died and gone to heaven."

When people entered the fortieth-anniversary Ruby Jubilee Festival, this is the phrase Karey and Nancy heard most often. Over and over, people saw "heaven" as they looked to the ceiling and saw an enormous circular installation of approximately one hundred red-and-white quilts. The walls all around were also filled with red-and-white quilts. It was a stunning exhibition and a fitting celebration: a true jubilee.

The inspiration for this show came from an exhibition held in New York City in 2011. For that show, collector Joanna S. Rose shared her 650 red-and-white quilts, and they all were hung in a giant space from swirling beams, almost as if the quilts were following a soaring roller coaster. It was triumphant. When the quilters saw the soaring height and

A beautiful collection of red-and-white quilts on display in 2014.

sheer volume of red-and-white quilts in Houston in 2014, they felt the same thrill.

Quilter, curator, and fabric designer Jamie Fingal put it plain and simple: "Nobody hangs a show like Quilts Inc. Karey respects quilts and that makes all the difference." Forty years of experience and love for quilts led to this tour de force of exhibitions. For those who were there, it was unforgettable.

Can You Quilt in Outer Space? Karen Nyberg Did

In 2013, International Quilt Festival partnered with NASA—yes, NASA. Astronaut Karen Nyberg was the flight engineer on Expeditions 36 and 37 to the International Space Station (ISS), where she spent a total of 180 days in space. During her mission in 2013, Karen sewed a stuffed toy dinosaur for her son Jack (who was three years old at the time) and stitched a small Texas flag for her astronaut husband, Doug Hurley.

Karen also happens to be a quilter, and as she was about to take off for her second journey in space, she agreed to sew a star-themed quilt block while in orbit. Sewing just one block would be a fairly simple task for most quilters on earth, but imagine trying to cut and sew fabric while you are weightless and with very limited tools. Clearly it's not a good idea to take a rotary cutter to space. But Karen did, in fact, sew her block in space, and she partnered with Festival to issue a challenge to quilters. While still aboard the ISS, Karen filmed a short video inviting quilters to join her and make their own star-themed blocks. In the video, her long hair spreads in every direction while she floats around in zero gravity holding a microphone and her finished quilt block. Quilters were invited to send their blocks to be combined with Nyberg's for a quilt to debut at the 2014 event. Over 2,200 blocks were sent in, and Quilts Inc. staff and volunteers, led by Vicki Mangum, spent many long hours making them into not one quilt, but twenty-eight.

Karen's leadership by showing the world that she was a professional woman—an astronaut!—who also made quilts was a powerful moment in quilt history. Karey and Nancy felt privileged to welcome her to Festival.

Over 2,200 blocks were sent in to Quilts Inc. following NASA astronaut Karen Nyberg's historic sewing-in-space adventure aboard the International Space Station. The one block Karen Nyberg sewed in space is featured in the center of this quilt.

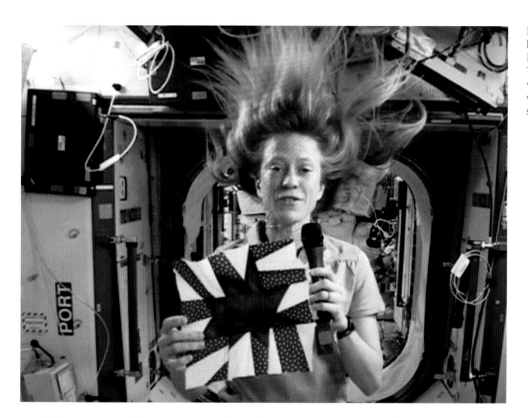

Karen Nyberg spent five and a half months aboard the International Space Station. This image is captured from the video she filmed aboard the ISS while holding the block she sewed in space.

Karen Nyberg made a special guest appearance at the 2014 Festival and shared her story with quilters.

Festival staff and volunteers spent hours constructing quilts from the 2,200 blocks submitted after Karen Nyberg (while flying aboard the International Space Station) invited quilters to make a quilt with her.

Texas Quilt Museum: Cementing a Legacy

by Sandra Sider, PhD, museum curator

For many years, Karey and Nancy dreamed of establishing a museum in Texas to recognize and celebrate the art and beauty of quilts, the creativity of their makers, and the continuing contributions of quiltmaking to history and culture. A fortuitous visit to the small Texas town of La Grange was the catalyst that made the dream a reality. They discovered two historic 1890s buildings right in the center of town—formerly a hardware store and a furniture store—and immediately knew that these old buildings would make an excellent spot for a museum.

Karey and Nancy decided to establish the Texas Quilt Museum in La Grange, which is in Fayette County and within easy driving distance of Houston, Austin, and San Antonio. Significant restoration of the two buildings was required. By breaking through the common wall, the cofounders created more than ten thousand square feet of space. After many months of repairs and restoration, the Texas Quilt Museum galleries, with their high ceilings, brick walls, and original hardwood floors, comprise a fine showcase both for antique and contemporary quilt art.

While the state of Texas is obviously part of the museum's name, the scope is certainly international. Karey and Nancy, as cofounders and codirectors, have committed significant levels of donated professional time and material support to ensure a strong foundation for operating a sustainable art-educational institution. This effort includes access to the International Quilt Festival Collection for exhibitions, plus business planning, marketing, and publicity support; curatorial expertise; and educational-programming staff. In its first few years, the Texas Quilt Museum benefited from economic development grants totaling $50,000 from the City of La Grange, and currently the Texas Commission on the Arts provides significant funding.

Recognizing Research with "Bybee Scholar" Honor

In 2014, the Texas Quilt Museum established its Bybee Scholar program, which recognizes those who are committed to the study of quilts and quilting history, directly supporting the museum's mission. The award is presented on behalf of the Faith P. and Charles L. Bybee Foundation and the Texas Quilt Museum. Recipients of this annual award (as of 2019) are Teresa Duryea Wong, Katherine J. Adams, Kathy Moore, Marcia Kaylakie, and Marian Ann Montgomery, Ph.D.

In addition to this growing list of Bybee Scholars, other artists, quilters, and writers who visit the museum inevitably take away an expanded view of quilts and a more profound knowledge of the art form. They also have the opportunity to study quilts and quilt history in the Pearce Memorial Library and Material Culture Study Center, with more than 6,500 items cataloged.

Texas Quilt Museum in La Grange, Texas.

Curating Flowers

The institution's impact on the immediate community of La Grange extends beyond the museum walls with Grandmother's Flower Garden, a period garden including an arbor, gazebo, and benches in the large lot adjacent to the museum. Everyone can enjoy the monumental quilt mural painted on the museum's exterior as locals gather in this cultural hub for lunch and conversation. Fayette County residents also enjoy a free day once a year to view the exhibitions, and all museum lectures are free to the public. Numerous groups of schoolchildren have visited, and the museum has begun to offer gallery tours via Skype to schools. Our global community of visitors to the museum extends around the world, embracing fifty-eight countries as well as every state in the US.

Exhibitions

As of the spring 2018 season, the museum has displayed more than 1,400 quilts in sixty exhibitions, with four exhibition seasons annually that balance art quilts with antique/vintage examples and contemporary traditional quilts. Curated shows have presented quilts by Teresa Barkley, Sue Benner, Hazel Canny, Cynthia Collier, Judith Content, Jane Dunnewold, Caryl Bryer Fallert-Gentry, Yukiko Hirano, Terrie Hancock Mangat, and Susan Shie. Group shows have included several Studio Art Quilt Associates (SAQA) global exhibitions along with SAQA regional exhibitions. In 2014, the museum published *Butterflies and Their Beautiful Kin*, a catalog documenting the first exhibition juried exclusively for the institution, and has launched a monograph series written by the

museum curator concerning quilts exhibited by featured studio artists.

The Texas Quilt Museum was founded in November 2010 as a 510(c)(3) nonprofit and officially opened on November 13, 2011. The museum welcomes visitors from Thursday through Sunday. The museum store offers a wide range of gifts, from whimsical T-shirts to textile-related unique works of art. In addition, the store offers antique and contemporary quilts for sale that have been donated to benefit the Texas Quilt Museum. The architecture firm that led the restoration of the two original, historic buildings won the statewide Texas Historic Preservation Award in 2012 for their work on the Texas Quilt Museum.

Top left: Quilters demonstrate hand-quilting techniques at Festival, 1998.

Right: Shoppers at the twentieth anniversary of International Quilt Festival in 1994.

Bottom left: Beloved quilter and teacher Libby Lehman teaches an eager group of quilters in 1999.

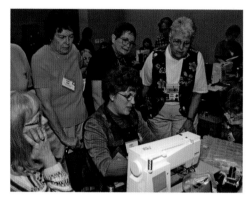

Shannon Conley. *S is for . . . #3: You Cleared My Name*. 2012. Wide variety of commercial fabrics: 70" × 30" (178 × 76 cm). Embellished with twine, trim, wool roving, beads, polymer clay, dryer sheets, and paint sticks. Machine quilted.

Exhibited at Festival in 2013 in the special exhibit *A Walk in the Wild*, sponsored by Studio Art Quilt Associates of New Mexico. It was once believed that this species ate dinosaurs, but new discoveries have proved otherwise. Shannon Conley is both an artist and a scientist, and she made this quilt in honor of the scientific research that cleared *Coelophysis bauri* of cannibalism.

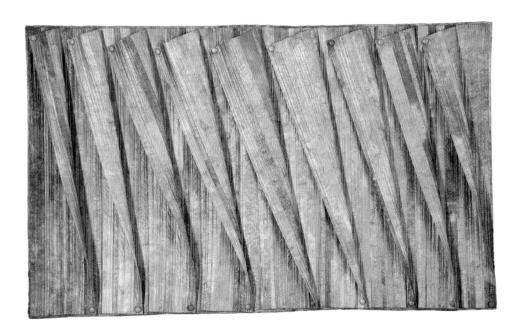

Anna Hergert. *The Sky in Monet's Garden—Sunrise to Sunset*. 2007. 42" × 68" (107 × 173 cm). Machine quilted.

Included in the Festival special exhibit *Sky's the Limit* in 2007. *Courtesy of International Quilt Festival Collection*

Pam Holland. *Heartache, Heritage and Happiness*. 2003.

Awarded the International Quilt Association's That Patchwork Place Best of Show in 2003. *Courtesy of International Quilt Festival Collection*

Sue Bleiweiss. *Tutti Frutti Village*. Cotton: 33" × 51" (84 × 129 cm). Machine quilted.

This colorful quilt won Honorable Mention in the International Quilt Association Art Whimsical category, 2012.

Top left: Before the Houston convention center was renovated in 2017, long lines for tickets for Festival were a common occurrence. Nowadays, buying advance tickets online is a common practice, and attendees can wait inside a large, spacious lobby.

Bottom left: This group of quilters is hand quilting on a large traditional frame. For some, this may be the first attempt at working in a traditional method, and they have pulled up a chair to practice and learn from experts. By 2000, when this photo was taken, machine quilting was by far the most popular method of quilt construction.

Right: This patriotic, wearable-art ensemble captured the attention of attendees at the 2002 Bernina Fashion Show.

Top left: Jean Evans. *Sun on Marty's Bike*. 2002. Awarded First Place in the IQA Art category, 2002.

Top right: Hollis Chatelain. *Innocence*. 2010. Cotton: 78" × 103" (185 × 262 cm). Hand dye-painted with thickened fiber reactive dyes, machine quilted.

Awarded the Viewer's Choice Award, sponsored by MamasLogHouseQuiltShop.com, 2010.

Enthusiastic quilters at the 2002 Festival.

Noriko Endo, from Japan, began teaching at Festival in 2003. Noriko Endo's classes are popular and fill up quickly with students eager to learn from this talented artist and generous teacher.

The 2017 Founder's Award went to this stunning traditional quilt, *Baltimore in Bloom*, by Sally Magee. This meticulous appliqué and the beautiful palette combine for a dramatic effect.

Hollis Chatelain began teaching at Festival in 1998 and has taught every year since then. In 2018, she celebrated twenty years of teaching at Festival. This photo was taken in her classroom at the 2002 Festival.

Arlene Blackburn. *Midnight in the Garden of Good and Elvis*. 2002.

This quilt holds a certain fame in International Quilt Festival history, and unfortunately it is not a happy story. In 2002, a man who was an exhibitor at Festival (this individual will remain unnamed here because he does not deserve recognition) was conducting questionable business deals and was in a legal dispute with Arlene Blackburn. One evening, after the show closed, he filled a water bottle with bleach and walked right up to Arlene's quilt *Midnight in the Garden of Good and Elvis* and threw bleach on it. The second photo shows the quilt immediately after the incident.

It is a painful memory for Arlene. She does not want to be remembered as the person whose quilt was ruined by bleach. Arlene eventually constructed an all-new replica of the ruined quilt. As for Festival organizers, this incident prompted a thorough review of security measures and some minor improvements. That said, because this individual was wearing a badge indicating he was an exhibitor, there was no reason for the security personnel who were stationed nearby to suspect anything unusual. The perpetrator of this crime served time in prison. The author would like to thank Arlene and Karey for allowing the before-and-after images of this heartbreaking part of Festival history to be published.

Julie Silber, pictured at the right, is a well-respected dealer of antique quilts, and her booth at Festival each year is always popular. In fact, International Quilt Festival is one of the premier destinations for antique quilts for sale under one roof. The shoppers in this photo are studying an Amish-designed quilt in 2002.

Cynthia England is pictured in front of *Open Season*, which won the IQA That Patchwork Place Best of Show award in 2000. She spent six years making this quilt, using techniques she devised herself. The quilt contains over twenty-one thousand individual pieces and is made of 280 different fabrics.

Special exhibit *It's Raining Cats and Dogs*, 2014.

Megan Farkas. *Sakura I: Hanaogi Views the Cherry Blossoms*. 2010. Cotton, silk, silk flowers, glass beads: 60" × 98" (152 × 249 cm). Hand appliqué, hand embroidery, hand quilted.

This quilt was inspired by a woodblock print from ca. 1795 by Chokosai Eisho. In 2011 it was awarded the Future of Quilting Award, sponsored by Tin Lizzie 18.

Janet Steadman. *Dream Fields*. 2010. Hand-dyed fabric. Machine pieced, machine quilted.

Colors and shapes seem to float effortlessly in this innovative quilt. IQA awarded it Third Place in the Art-Abstract Large category sponsored by Hoffman Fabrics, 2012.

Left: Kathy Nakajima (a.k.a. Yachiyo Katsuno) lives in Japan, where she is well known for her gorgeous, colorful Hawaiian-style quilts. This quilt is titled *Sunshine Rose Garden* and was awarded the Founders Award, sponsored by International Quilt Festival, 2003.

Right: Cindy Cooksey. *The Innkeeper Wore Black*. 40" × 40" (102 × 102 cm). Machine quilted.

Exhibited in the *Dinner at Eight* special exhibition, 2016, curated by Jamie Fingal and Leslie Tucker Jenison. The show was an invitation-only, juried exhibition, 2009–2018. As of 2017, only one artist has been included in every show: Cindy Cooksey.

Cassandra Williams. *River Run*. 37" × 69" (94 × 175 cm). Raw-edge appliqué, machine pieced, machine quilted.

This unique quilt features an original design with a natural underwater setting and fish. It won First Place in the Pictorial category, sponsored by FreeSpirit Fabrics, 2002. It was also awarded the Judge's Choice by Joen Wolfrom, sponsored by Roxanne Products.

Left: These quilts were part of the *Lone Stars III* exhibit, which highlighted quilts from the state of Texas made between 1986 and 2011.

Right: These children are learning simple sewing and quilting skills at Festival, 2015. One hopes that they will one day grow up to become Dedicated Quilters.

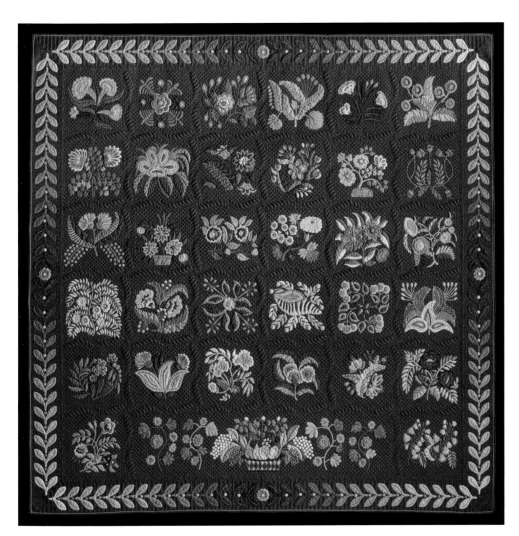

Barbara Korengold. *Zeruah's Legacy*. 2013. Cotton: 79" × 77" (201 × 195 cm). Hand appliqué, hand quilted.

This quilt was inspired by the *Zeruah Guernsey Caswell* carpet in the collection of the Metropolitan Museum of Art in New York City. It was awarded the 2014 IQA Founder's Award.

Two large-scale portraits command the viewer's eye. On the left is a quilt titled *Portrait Noir* by Trish Morris-Plise, a self-portrait with the names of important people, events, and places in the artist's life stitched into the quilt. Quilted by Sandra Bruce. On the right is a quilt titled *Chuck Close Two* by Sandra Bruce. It is hand appliquéd, machine pieced, painted, and machine quilted and contains 1,050 two-inch squares of fabric. 2016 Festival.

A smiling Alex Anderson and Ricky Tims are pictured at Festival. They are the hosts of "The Quilt Show with Alex Anderson and Ricky Tims," which is multiplatform and includes a popular online TV program. Many quilters consider landing an interview or demonstration spot on "The Quilt Show" as a major coup for their quilting career.

The Piece Corps is an elite group of volunteers who spend an inordinate amount of time and energy preparing for Festival and ensuring that each and every quilt on display is executed with perfection. A few of the volunteers are pictured here working behind the scenes as they help get the show ready for the public in 2014.

Most people think of fabric when they think of quilt shopping, but thread is big business too. As of 2014, the Dedicated Quilter spent an average of $158 annually on thread and had approximately $800 worth of thread in her collection. Shoppers are seen here collecting their favorite type and color of thread.

Above left: Jennifer Day. *Holy Cow*.

Jennifer Day bought her first sewing machine in 2010 and began making art quilts by covering an image of a photograph printed on fabric in thread. Just eighteen months later, she was awarded the "Spirit of Texas" award by IQA at the 2011 International Quilt Festival for this poignant quilt.

Above right: This showstopper was the third quilt by Cynthia England to win an IQA Handi Quilter Best of Show award in 2016. Cynthia spent over one year creating *Reflections of Cape Town*, and it is constructed with 8,400 individual pattern pieces in it.

Junko Fujiwara. *Fantastic!* Awarded the 2017 Founders Award.

Left: Teacher Karen Kay Buckley in her classroom at Festival in 2010.

Right: Masa Yanagimoto, from Takamatsu, Kagawa, Japan, shows off the back of her quilt titled *Pray for the Land of Green*, which was awarded Second Place in the Mixed Technique category in the IQA competition at the 2013 Festival.

True to its international roots, attendees at Festival will find exhibitors from all over the world who offer an incredible variety of textiles, fabric, and even handmade baskets and dozens of other unique cultural items. This photo is from the 2010 Festival.

For one special night, members of the International Quilt Association gather for their annual awards ceremony. In a dramatic fashion, the quilts that win the most-prestigious awards are kept hidden behind a black curtain. One by one, the curtain falls as each winner's name is announced. Once all the awards have been announced, the quilt paparazzi pop up out of their chairs and rush over to take photos of the stunning award winners. This photo is from 2014.

Some viewers spend hours studying the quilts on view at Festival. The seemingly endless displays of quilts of every kind provide a visual treat. Quilters are often inspired to go home and try new techniques or make new quilts after viewing these diverse exhibitions.

Gail Smith. *Sarah's Revival in Blue*. 2015. Cotton: 87" × 84" (221 × 213 cm). Hand appliqué, machine quilted by Karen McTavish. Based on a pattern by Sue Garman.

Gail Smith currently lives in Chicago, but she lived in Houston for two years (in the 1980s), and she quickly found her way to Great Expectations, the quilt shop owned by Karey Patterson Bresenhan. She took classes and attended Festival during her time in Houston. She put her quilting aside to raise (and homeschool) her seven children and finally picked it back up again in 2005. Her passion is hand appliqué, and it certainly shows in this stunning two-color quilt.

Linda Roy. *Subtle Sixties*. 2004. Cotton: 81.5" × 82". Pieced, hand appliqué, hand embroidery, machine quilted.

Linda used an unusual technique for this quilt: she created a swirling design, executed by hand embroidery, on top of the quilting stitches. The result is a beautiful, highly creative quilt with a traditional motif. It was awarded the IQA Founder's Award in 2004.

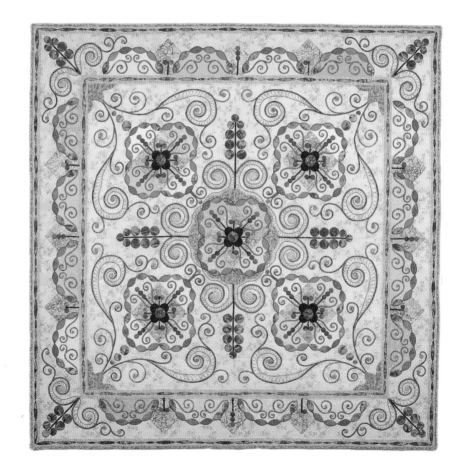

Suzan Engler. *Somebody Say Treat?* 2013. Cotton: 32" × 32" (81 × 81 cm). Digital manipulation of photographs placed on a digitally created background, printed on cotton fabric and heavily stitched.

Exhibited in *It's Raining Cats and Dogs*, 2013.

Linda Anderson. *Velvet Flowers*. 2017. Cotton: 30.5" × 50.5" (77 × 128 cm). Jacquard textile paint, raw-edge appliqué, hand-painted pieces, machine quilted.

The International Quilt Association awarded *Velvet Flowers* the Gammill Master Award for Contemporary Artistry in 2018.

Linda attended her first International Quilt Festival in 2017. She represents the latest generation of quilters who are still discovering the magic and mystery of this special event and who are turning all that inspiration into beautiful quilts.

The Steel Magnolias

Long before the popular 1989 movie with the all-star cast, the term "steel magnolia" referred to a rarified group of southern women. A steel magnolia was simultaneously tough and feminine. Karey and Nancy are true steel magnolias.

This description of them came up again and again by people interviewed for this book. These individuals spoke of their southern charm and sweet smiles and, in the same breath, were in awe of the duo's business savvy, fairness, and determination. While working together with unwavering trust and support for each other, they've set the bar high and inspired millions to make and love quilts.

These steel magnolias changed the course of quilt history. They taught all of us that quilts are important, that all quilts matter, and, even more so, that the makers matter too. The quilts we love and the quilts we make are worth preserving and are an important part of our history. We are not anonymous. We are quilters.

Partners, cousins, founders, and collectors. So many meaningful descriptors can be used to describe the contributions of Nancy O'Bryant Puentes and Karey Patterson Bresenhan.